WHITE PRIVI...

The myth of a post-racial society

Kalwant Bhopal

First published in Great Britain in 2018 by

Policy Press
University of Bristol
1-9 Old Park Hill
Bristol
BS2 8BB
UK
t: +44 (0)117 954 5940
pp-info@bristol.ac.uk
www.policypress.co.uk

North America office:
Policy Press
c/o The University of Chicago Press
1427 East 60th Street
Chicago, IL 60637, USA
t: +1 773 702 7700
f: +1 773 702 9756
sales@press.uchicago.edu
www.press.uchicago.edu

© Policy Press 2018

British Library Cataloguing in Publication Data
A catalogue record for this book is available from the British Library.

Library of Congress Cataloging-in-Publication Data
A catalog record for this book has been requested.

ISBN 978-1-4473-3597-9 paperback
ISBN 978-1-4473-3599-3 ePub
ISBN 978-1-4473-3600-6 Mobi
ISBN 978-1-4473-3598-6 ePdf

The right of Kalwant Bhopal to be identified as the author of this work has been
asserted by her in accordance with the Copyright, Designs and Patents Act 1988.

Cover design by Andrew Corbett
Printed and bound in Great Britain by TJ International,
Padstow
Policy Press uses environmentally responsible print
partners

MIX
Paper from
responsible sources
FSC® C013056

"More than ever, the study of whiteness proves indispensable. Kalwant Bhopal is a voice of reason in a cacophony of fervor. She takes to task the presumptions of post-raciality and defies its pretenders. We will be post-racial in a condition of post-racism. Until then, evidence and ethics are on her side."
Zeus Leonardo, University of California, Berkeley, author of *Race Frameworks: A Multidimensional Theory of Racism and Education*

"A lucid straightforward illumination of whiteness and white privilege, as it is currently acted-out in school and society, despite social justice policies. It puts before readers the pervasiveness and meanness of white privilege in education/schooling and society in this neoliberal, non-post-racial era. Timely and deserving of urgent attention."
Carl A. Grant, University Wisconsin-Madison and author of *Du Bois and Education*

"Offers a crucial and timely focus on the perpetuation of white privilege in a society that claims to be post-racial, and the continuing disadvantages experienced by black and minority ethnic groups ... provides a wealth of data on social, educational and economic inequalities in both the UK and USA where white supremacist hate is increasing. It should be read by policy makers, practitioners and the public to help them realise how white privilege works and disadvantage is perpetuated."
Sally Tomlinson, University of Oxford

"In this wide-ranging book Bhopal addresses racial inequality in Britain and the United States. She demonstrates how racial inequality is pervasive in British society across sectors, especially education and the labor market, an important perspective for scholars. A great introduction to issues of racial inequality."
Natasha Kumar Warikoo, Harvard University

To my children:

Dylan, Yasmin, Deva and Sachin.

Thank you.

Contents

List of figures and tables

Figures

Tables

Acknowledgements

There are many people who have contributed to the ideas expressed in this book. I would like to thank my colleagues and friends who have engaged with me in stimulating discussions about Brexit, Trump, racism, whiteness and anything else I needed either a second opinion on or just needed to talk about. Huge thanks to Martin Dyke, Michael Tomlinson, Tony Kelly, John Preston, Ross Deuchar and Ian McGimpsey. Massive thanks to my friends across the pond for their discussions about Trump, racism and whiteness in the US: Carl Grant, Alex Allweiss, Thandeka Chapman and all the graduate students at the University of Wisconsin-Madison, where I spent part of my sabbatical in 2016. Mid-way through the writing of this book I was appointed Professorial Research Fellow in the Centre for Research in Race and Education, School of Education at the University of Birmingham. I could not have imagined the opportunities this role has given me. I am truly grateful to my colleagues at the University of Birmingham and the School of Education for their support. I would especially like to thank David Gillborn and Claire E. Crawford, my colleagues in the Centre for Research in Race and Education, for their support, feedback and critical engagement, which has enabled me to sharpen and refine my scholarship.

Many of the ideas expressed in this book have been presented at numerous conferences and seminars, which have always been interesting and engaging experiences. However, sometimes I have experienced hostility and aggression about my views on whiteness, racism and white privilege. I am grateful for all the feedback I have received, both positive and negative, because it has confirmed the existence and predominance of white privilege as expressed in this book.

Thanks to Alison Shaw for inviting me to write this book and for all her support – it has been a pleasure. And thanks to everyone at Policy Press for the smooth process, especially Rebecca Tomlinson, Jess Mitchell and Kathryn King. I am especially grateful to the anonymous reviewers for their insightful, thoughtful and constructive comments on the manuscript – which have strengthened the arguments and coherency of the book. Thanks also to the participants who allowed me to use their stories. The inaccuracies in the book (if there are any) are all mine.

Massive thanks to my partner in crime Martin Myers for his continued and unquestioning support and for reading several drafts of the entire manuscript and providing brilliant comments – as always. And to my four wonderful children – Dylan, Yasmin, Deva and Sachin – thanks for always making me realise what truly is important. I hope your future is a better one.

A personal note

This book is about racism. I am the daughter of immigrants. I grew up in a working class family. None of my parents went to university and both my parents worked in manual labour jobs in factories. I was the first in my family to attend university and I attended my local post-1992 university. Neither my parents nor I had any idea that there were different types of universities or that there were hierarchies of universities. Had fees been introduced I would never have gone to university, because my parents simply could not have afforded it. My parents came over from India to England over 50 years ago for a better life. I was the first of my siblings to be born here in England and I consider myself British. However, from an early age it was apparent that I would never be accepted as British in white England. I remember as a child my dad regularly being stopped by police because he was 'a Paki in a flash car'. Aged 10 I recall being spat in the face by a girl and boy in my primary school and told I was a 'smelly Paki'. From an early age I realised that I would always be judged by the colour of my skin and nothing else. This has carried on. In one organisation I worked in I was racially bullied for several years by a white female. I left the organisation but she has since been promoted to a senior role. I still continue to experience racism, often on a daily basis, but it is more subtle and nuanced and I will continue to name racism regardless of the negative repercussions of doing so. In this book I outline how racism continues to marginalise and exclude black and minority ethnic people, but I also explore some of the ways we can move forward to ensure that we are no longer judged by the colour of our skin. My four children give me so much hope. Racism, social justice and equality often feature in our dinner-time conversations. They continue to tell me how much more accepting and inclusive their generation are of difference, and that in the future people will no longer be judged by the colour of their skin. I hope they are right.

Cambridge, Massachusetts, November 2017

Foreword

Inherited privilege is both actual status and curious state of mind. Some men and women accumulate wealth, influence and stature. They feel entitled and deserving, disdain those below them. Donald Trump is the latest icon of this social Darwinism as is the Tory throwback, Jacob Rees Mogg. There will be plenty more after them. Are such human behaviours and inequalities an unavoidable part of all social configurations? Or should they be thought of as by-products of certain economic systems, histories, beliefs, distortions and competitiveness? Privilege is all that and imperceptibly more.

As humans we have consciousness, the ability to absorb information, analyse and assess situations, to deliberate. Yet most of the secure and fortunate remain oblivious of their positions. Privilege is never consciously recognised or defined. It is normalised, internalised, maintained, diffuse. Facts, figures and challenges provoke vehement denial. Think of it as a collective mental block.

Bequeathed advantages are found in every nation, among almost all ethnic and racial types. In East Africa, where I was born, Asians were richer and thought they were genetically superior to black Africans. That is still the case today, long after independence. Meanwhile, in oil rich Middle Eastern states, Arabs see themselves as the permanently blessed and South Asians as lowly, dispensable inferiors.

However, from the age of exploration, when Europeans set off in search of new lands and profits, to the post-communist era of aggressive Western capitalism, white privilege has been dominant across the globe. Furthermore, through the centuries, relentless Caucasian expansionism and hubris persuaded large numbers of non-white peoples of their own unworthiness. You see 'native' humbleness in almost every developing country. Aid agencies, tourist companies, big Western businesses and Christian missions in the 21st century all perpetuate the pernicious notion that white men and women are more evolved and of a higher order than the rest of humanity. The good news is that we may be coming to the end of this long period of settled racial omnipotence. The bad news is that a cataclysmic culture war has only just begun.

White people, from the most to the least powerful, feel beleaguered. The ground beneath their feet trembles. India and China are becoming stupendously productive and assertive. In 2018, the Indian economy is expected to grow by 7.5 per cent and China's by even more. Within Western nations, indigenous citizens feel demographically endangered as their numbers fall while immigrants with high birth rates 'take over'. These are primeval fears of survival, not in the usual sense of life over death, but the hitherto unconquerable might and right of whiteness. That currency is now devalued and causing much disorientation.

Unsurprisingly, we are witnessing much rage and retaliatory charges. Listen to the howls. White people – middle-class men most of all – claim to be real victims of black racism and 'ethnic' takeovers, of PC GONE MAD, of Feminazis, Islamicists and other lethal, anti-Western forces. These grievances explain the Trump victory, Brexit, drift to the hard right in Europe and Australia.

The sense of jeopardy is exacerbated by the rising, worldwide resistance to the latest incarnation of capitalism – as rabid and unforgiving as that which swept across the east after the 16th century. After the Berlin Wall fell, the West thought it had won the ideological battles. As the US political economist Francis Fukuyama boasted, it was the end of history. Didn't quite turn out that way. In the last decade the model has been condemned by citizens from east to west, north to south. Millions now believe it reinforces and justifies extreme inequality. They want a better, fairer system.

In Kalwant Bhopal's book, modern manifestations of racism and racial privilege are located within the neoliberal economic structure. Such analysis is rare and necessary if one is to understand how in a world we were told was globalised, white people are still perpetually more advantaged than men, women and children of colour.

Yasmin Alibhai-Brown

ONE

Introduction: race as disadvantage

This book focusses on exploring how race operates as a form of disadvantage in modern-day society. It argues that individuals from black and minority ethnic backgrounds, by virtue of their racial identity, are positioned as outsiders in a society that values whiteness and 'white privilege'. The main argument of the book is that within a neoliberal context policy making in its attempt to be inclusive has portrayed an image of a post-racial society, when in reality vast inequalities between white and black and minority ethnic communities continue to exist. Policy making has exacerbated rather than addressed the inequalities which result from processes of racism, exclusion and marginalisation in which white identities are prioritised and privileged above all others.

The concept of neoliberalism is a contested and complex term that generally refers to the systemic privileging of a 'free market' as the mechanism best suited to manage the movement of all capital, goods and services, including services that would conventionally be understood to be public services. Neoliberalism is therefore associated with the drive to privatise public services such as education and healthcare and the disposal of assets owned by the state to private investors. While critics of neoliberal policies often portray such movements as the erosion of a 'public' or 'common' good, neoliberals would suggest such marketisation fosters greater individualism and responsibility. This book will explore how policy making within a neoliberal context works to protect whiteness and disadvantage those from black and minority ethnic groups.

1

What is neoliberalism?

The concept of neoliberalism has been used in different ways but it has mainly been incorporated into economic frameworks, policies and thinking. In some respects neoliberalism can be understood as a type of liberalism. Olssen states:

> neoliberalism reinforces many of the central axioms of classical liberalism. It reinforces those pertaining to the relations between the individual and society, the conception of freedom, the view of the self as a rational utility maximiser, the view of the distinction between public and private spheres as separate, and the rejection of any conception of a public good over and above the aggregate sum of individual ends.[1]

Other definitions of neoliberalism include it being defined as

> an ensemble of economic and social policies, forms of governance, and discourses and ideologies that promote individual self-interest, unrestricted flows of capital, deep reductions in the cost of labour and sharp retrenchment of the public sphere. Neoliberals champion privatisation of social goods and withdrawal of government from provision for social welfare on the premise that competitive markets are more effective and efficient.[2]

Has neoliberalism worked?

Neoliberal policy making has had a significant effect on policy making in all areas of life. However, in its quest to promote self-interests, which is masked as giving individuals more choice and opportunity to take control over their own lives, it has in effect created less choice and less opportunity. For example the Conservative 1988 Reform Act, which introduced choice via open enrolment, enabled parents to 'express a preference' for schools. This was followed by a White Paper, in 1992, titled 'Choice and Diversity', which cemented in a 1992 Education (schools) Act. New Labour under Blair continued the policy. This gave the illusion that parents could have greater influence over where they sent their children to school, but this only applied to those from middle-class backgrounds who were able to use their social, cultural and economic capital to either send their children to private schools or to move to areas where there were high-performing schools. Consequently, 'school choice' favoured the middle classes and worked to reinforce divisions based on class and indeed race. As a result, families with low incomes and those from black and minority ethnic[3] backgrounds are left to accept their local schools, which are seen as 'bad' and not performing well in league tables. Robertson suggests that '[t]he proxy for quality where the school is in the league tables, not only opens up or closes off access to further privileges, but it produces the system of social stratification'.[4]

Neoliberal policy making is a way of reorganising society in which educational sites, such as schools and universities, become sites that are based on entrepreneurship, value for money and profit. Robertson suggests that neoliberalism is a class project that has three specific aims. These are:

> (i) the redistribution of wealth upward to the ruling elites through new structures of governance; (ii) transformation of education systems so that the production of workers for the economy is the primary mandate; and (iii) breaking down of education as a public sector monopoly, opening it up to strategic investment by for profit firms. To be realistic, all three aims must break down the institutional interests of teachers, trade unions and fractions [sic] of civil society who have supported the idea of education as a public good and public sector, and as an intrinsic element of the state-civil-society social contract.[5]

Neoliberalism also paved the way for a system of profit and consequently exploitation of labour. A new model of education included funding linked to outcomes, the introduction of league tables to create a competitive environment between schools, pressure to increase performance with performance being measured and a justification of how money is spent in schools.

There is evidence to suggest that neoliberal policy making has not delivered in producing greater equality and reducing poverty; rather there is evidence to suggest a slow-down in economic growth and an increase in inequality and poverty in some parts of the world.[6]

Davies and Bansel suggest that

> [t]he emergence of neoliberal states has been characterised by the transformation of the administrative state, one previously responsible for human well-being, as well as for the economy, into a state that gives power to global corporations and installs apparatuses and knowledges through which people are reconfigured as productive economic entrepreneurs of their own lives.[7]

The authors suggest that individuals themselves have a false sense of power and freedom and this has manifested in a collective lack of responsibility, which has allowed unions to have less power in society. 'Individual subjects have thus welcomed this increasing individualism as a sign of their freedom and at the same time, institutions have increased competition, responsibilisation and the transfer of risk from the state to individuals at a heavy cost to many individuals and indeed to many nations'.[8]

Neoliberalism and race

Goldberg[9] refers to racial neoliberalism as a process that has resulted in a structural shift in racial governance, which has become legitimised through policy making. In the UK this has taken place through the introduction of anti-terror legislation such as the teaching of 'British values' and the Prevent agenda[10] (which I discuss in Chapter Five). In this book I argue that within a neoliberal context, policy making has failed in its attempts to champion inclusion and social justice, and in doing so has further marginalised the position of black and minority ethnic groups. Rather, within this context, policy making has worked to reinforce the position of whites at the expense of disadvantaging those from black and minority ethnic backgrounds. Such policy making works to further perpetuate a society in which whiteness is privileged and prioritised. All of the chapters in this book provide evidence to suggest that within a neoliberal context policy making works to disadvantage those from black and minority ethnic groups and reinforce whiteness and white identity. Policy making is legitimised through a process and rhetoric that emphasises the benefits of neoliberalism to all, yet there is clear evidence, as I present in this book, to suggest that within the neoliberal context policy making reinforces white privilege.

The belief in a meritocracy (which I discuss in Chapter Six on higher education) is an example of the failure of policy making within the context of neoliberalism – that those who rise to the top have done so because they have worked hard and deserve to be there, in comparison to those who have not – who are lazy. Neoliberalism reinforces the importance of access to the social networks, mentoring, patronage and power that whiteness brings, and it works on the premise that inequality does not necessarily perpetuate disadvantages in social structures (such as poverty, wealth and income). Neoliberalism fails to acknowledge racism by reinforcing the notion that neoliberalism is for the good of the whole of society, rather than a select few. Yet the evidence presented in this book suggests this is not the case.

Outline of the book

In the following chapters I explore different aspects of whiteness and white privilege. In each of these I discuss how whiteness and white privileges work to serve the interests of whites at the expense of those from black and minority ethnic backgrounds. In Chapter Two, exploring white privilege, I discuss how whiteness and white identities operate as a form of privilege in society. Whiteness and white privilege are explored in two different political and social contexts, those of the UK and the US. Despite great historical, cultural and social differences between these two countries, many black and minority ethnic groups remain marginalised at different levels of society in which white identities predominate.

Chapter Three, 'Not white enough', argues that particular kinds of whiteness – which I refer to as acceptable and non-acceptable forms of whiteness – are privileged and protected. Acceptable forms of whiteness are based on the perception of conforming to society's expectations. Within these divisions, other forms of hierarchies further distinguish different forms of whiteness and these are based on language, dress and taste. Non-acceptable and non-legitimate forms of whiteness are based on the positioning of white minority groups such as Gypsies and Travellers[11] who live in the UK.

In Chapter Four, 'Intersectionality: gender, race and class', I examine how class and gender play a key role in the positioning of black and minority ethnic women in society and discuss the experiences of black and Asian women in relation to how stereotypes operate to marginalise and exclude some groups over others. I provide case study examples of Asian women in the UK and black African American men in the US to examine how race, gender and class impact on the experiences of non-white women working in universities in the UK and the US.

Chapter Five, 'Race, schooling and exclusion', explores how those from black and minority ethnic backgrounds in the UK and US are disadvantaged in their schooling experiences. The chapter draws on the experiences of black and minority ethnic teachers to explore how schools cater for some groups over others and in which exclusionary processes take place that disadvantage black and minority ethnic groups. The chapter argues that children's experience of schooling is affected by their race and, in turn, their class. It explores how UK education policy making has failed black and minority ethnic groups in its aims for an inclusive educational agenda.

Chapter Six, 'Higher education, race and representation', examines why black and minority ethnic groups remain under-represented in elite and Russell Group universities. It argues that processes of exclusionary practices take place in elite and Russell Group universities in which white privilege dominates to exclude those from non-white backgrounds. In this chapter I suggest that processes of exclusion based on race are used to maintain the elite position of universities, which are based on white, middle-class acceptance. Those from non-white and working-class backgrounds are excluded from such universities. As a result, such universities are able to maintain their position of privilege.

Chapter Seven, 'Racism and bullying in the UK', explores the failure of policy making and argues that equality policies operate to regulate public behaviour in which racist behaviours are unacknowledged. By drawing on two UK case studies, I suggest that whiteness and white identities are protected when complaints about racism are made. When such complaints are made, policies and attitudes within schools and universities fail to acknowledge the existence of such behaviour. As a result, a failure to acknowledge racist acts works to protect white identities and dismiss acts of racism.

Chapter Eight, 'Racial inequalities in the labour market', specifically explores how, through a process of racism, black and minority ethnic groups are less likely to occupy positions of power in the labour market. The chapter provides evidence showing how race works as a disadvantage in the labour market in which black and minority ethnic groups are more likely to be unemployed or in low-paid and insecure employment compared with their white counterparts. The chapter explores why ethnic inequalities in the labour market have persisted over time and examines why black and minority ethnic groups are on the one hand entering higher education in high numbers, yet on the other hand continue to experience unemployment and disadvantage in the labour market.

In Chapter Nine, 'Wealth, poverty and inequality', I examine how an increasing number of black and minority ethnic groups continue to live in low-income households, which affects their future life chances (such as access to higher education and the labour market). In this chapter I suggest that poverty and inequality are related to processes of racism, which has a significant impact on the future life choices and life chances of black and minority ethnic young people, both in the UK and the US.

In the final chapter, 'Conclusions: race, social justice and equality', I bring together previous discussions on race and suggest ways forward to engage with a social justice and inclusive agenda for change, in which the voices and lives of black and minority groups can be represented at all levels. I conclude that within a neoliberal context policy making has contributed to maintaining the status quo in which a post-racial society remains a myth, with covert and overt racism and racial exclusion continuing to operate at all levels and white identities remaining protected and privileged above all others.

The neoliberal shift and emphasis on the privatisation of goods and services has resulted in a dilution of the importance of inequalities such as race in society. The introduction of policy making within this context has masked the importance of race and rendered it insignificant. A rhetoric of a post-racial society in a post-Obama era has created a narrative in which race is no longer a problem. A silencing of race has resulted in the illusion that racial inequalities have been addressed and dealt with. Furthermore, the recent election of Donald J Trump as the 45th President of the United States of America will take race in a different direction, one in which race will be used to further marginalise and exclude those from black and minority ethnic backgrounds through rhetoric and policy making.

TWO

White privilege

In this chapter I discuss how whiteness and white identities operate as a form of privilege in society. Whiteness and white privilege are explored in two different political and social contexts, that of the UK and that of the US. Despite great historical, cultural and social differences between these two countries, many black and minority ethnic groups remain marginalised at different levels of society in which white identities predominate.

A recent report published by the Equalities and Human Rights Commission (EHRC)[1] found shocking evidence of the prevalence of racial inequalities in the UK; if you are from a black minority background you are three times more likely to be excluded from school, more likely to be unemployed, more likely to live in poverty, more likely to be physically restrained in police custody and more likely to be prosecuted and sentenced.[2] The EHRC argues:

> These inequalities are of significant concern. Not only do they mean that individuals are facing barriers in accessing jobs and services that impact on their ability to fulfil their potential, they also indicate that some parts of our community are falling behind and can expect poorer life changes than their neighbours. Multiple disadvantages result in social and economic exclusion for some groups and create tensions between communities, putting the 'haves' and 'have nots' in conflict.

The report also found a significant increase in the numbers of racist crimes in the last five years.[3]

Similarly in the US, if you are from a black African American background you are more likely to live in poverty (27% of black African Americans compared with 11% of all Americans), less likely to have a bachelor's degree and more likely to be stopped, searched and arrested than if you are from a white background.[4] Moreover, black African Americans are not only less likely to own their own homes now, they are also less likely to be the homeowners of the future; trends in home ownership suggest a slow but persistent year-on-year fall between 2005 and 2012 from 46% to 42.5%. Black African Americans have lower life expectancy than white Americans, they are less likely to have access to adequate health care and are more likely to be susceptible to diseases that they will die from.[5]

What seems remarkable is less the breadth of inequality, over very long periods of time, across the socio-political landscapes of two globally significant, liberal democratic nations, and more the feeling that such inequalities will persist in the future without any clear indication of change.

The British experience

When channel hopping between news bulletins or skimming newspaper stories, Britain in the 21st century often feels like a society overwhelmed by perceptions of insecurity and danger. Such accounts are fuelled by threats of terrorism or fears of an invasion of migrants and refugees. While such stories are often based on minimal or non-existent evidence, and perhaps because they tap into deeper but less easily understood 'feelings' of 'Britishness' and what constitutes a 'danger' to the British way of life, they have a tendency to reinforce deep-seated stereotypes, often racist stereotypes. Accounts of exotic foreigners threatening random acts of terrorism or displaced communities attempting to breach our borders do not just reinforce a feeling of their specific otherness, they also reinforce the otherness of black and non-white identities more generally. Black and non-white identities consequently become seen as another threatening element in a climate dominated by fear, terror and risk. Black identities have become associated with notions of danger and hostility, which pose a serious risk to disrupting harmony and stability in the UK.

In June 2016 the people of the UK were given the opportunity to have their say in whether to remain a member of the European Union. The result of this referendum was, against many expectations, that the electorate chose by a small majority to leave the EU. There were a number of immediate consequences to what has popularly become referred to as Brexit; these included a high level of political turmoil within the leadership of both major political parties and an immediate fall in the value of sterling. In addition to such political and economic consequences, it was also apparent that people's social lives had changed and their perception of what British identity might constitute changed quickly and irrevocably. For those pro-Europeans on the losing side this was often characterised in terms not just of disbelief at the decision, but also feelings of great abjection and despair for their futures. Newspaper headlines on the devastating result included 'Brexit: UK will lose £440 billion "derivatives industry" say global banks' (*The Independent*); 'City of London will suffer as a result of the EU referendum' (*The Independent*) and 'Small firms confidence sinks to lowest levels since Brexit' (*The Guardian*). Other headlines included, 'Britain is completely lost after Brexit and will beg for a deal, Brussels believes' (*The Telegraph*) and 'Pound plunges as "dramatic deterioration" in UK economy stokes Brexit recession' (*The Telegraph*). Unsurprisingly for the Brexiteers there was a great deal of jubilation in response to the result.

Another social change that appeared almost immediately to follow the decision to leave Europe was a significant rise in the reporting of hate crime. Two days after the result racist graffiti was scrawled across a Polish cultural centre in Hammersmith, West London.[6] Hammersmith and Fulham in London voted by 70%–30% to remain in the EU. Mrs Joanna Ciechanowska, who is director of the gallery in the Polish centre, said she did not think the graffiti incident would have happened before the referendum, 'but all of a sudden a small group of extremists feel empowered'. She went on to say, 'I hoped by a very small margin we'd stay in. But of course the hope was dashed. I think there was not enough clear information in the referendum campaign. All the broadcasts and the two main parties were appealing to people's emotions. It was all about immigration'.[7]

Similar accounts of racism emerged from all parts of the country. In Huntingdon, Cambridgeshire reports were made of laminated signs reading, 'Leave the EU: No more Polish vermin' being posted through the letterboxes of Polish families the day after the result. Other incidents include a Halal butchers being firebombed the day after Brexit, teenagers being filmed abusing a passenger on a Manchester tram, telling him to 'Get off the fucking tram now. Get Back to Africa' and migrants being told to 'fuck off back to your country'.[8]

True Vision, an organisation funded by the Metropolitan police, saw a 57% increase in the reporting of race crime between the Thursday and Sunday after the vote compared with the same period in the previous month. Other figures also suggest an increase in race crime since the referendum, with *Stop Hate UK* and *Tell Mama* both reporting increases.[9] Immigration was cited as one of the key reasons for voting to leave the European Union and the slogan 'we want our country back' was used to reinforce this message by Nigel Farage, leader of the UK Independence Party. Consequently, the result to leave gave individuals a legitimate right to voice their prejudices and racism towards minority ethnic groups. In this process Michael Keith (University of Oxford, Migration Research Centre) said, 'The unspeakable has become not only speakable, but commonplace'.[10]

Figure 2.1 shows the popular image used in the campaign of Nigel Farage standing beside a poster displaying crowds of non-white immigrants presumably trying to enter the UK.

Those who voted to leave the EU are more likely to be from the lowest social class (C2DE), have education that ended at secondary school level and are more likely to be from a white background.[11] The vote to leave was a clear indication of the predominance of whiteness. It was a reaction to mass immigration in which many white (working class) people felt they were being disadvantaged; immigrants were taking their jobs and were a strain on education and the National Health Service. And for once, they could have a voice in which they could use their vote as a legitimate platform to voice their racist views.

Brexit was an 'us versus them' vote in which white privilege was used at its most powerful – to separate out those who were *allowed to* belong and those who were *not*, and racism was used as a vehicle to promote this.

Figure 2.1: Breaking point: The EU has failed us all

US understandings of whiteness and identity

A conceptual understanding of whiteness, white identity and white privilege has been widely discussed in the US. Whiteness, white identity and white privilege are conceptualised and understood differently in the UK compared to the US; such understandings are affected by different social, historical and political climates.

The history of race relations in the US has been identified around struggles for equality and social justice, particularly in relation to the Civil Rights Movement. While fights for equal rights have advanced social justice issues – such as affirmative action – these have been significantly challenged . Recent events in the US have seen a return to overt racist acts, most markedly in the number of black men who have been shot by white police officers. In 2015 a total of 1,134 black men were killed by the US police, which was five times higher than white men of the same age.[12] A study carried out by *The Guardian* ('The Counted')[13] found that one in every 65 deaths of young African American males is a killing by the police. 'Despite making up only 2% of the total US population, African American males between the ages of 15 and 34 comprised more than 15% of all deaths logged this year [2015] by an ongoing investigation into the use of deadly force by police. Their rate of police-involved deaths was five times higher than for white men of the same age'.[14] The report also found that '[o]verall in 2015, black people were killed at twice the rate of white, Hispanic and native Americans. About 25% of the African Americans killed were unarmed, compared with 17% of white people'. The deaths of Michael Brown in Ferguson, Missouri – a black unarmed teenager who was shot by a white police officer – and the shooting of Tamir Rice – a 12-year-old who was carrying a toy gun – led to protests across the country accusing police officers of using unnecessary force against unarmed black African Americans. Recent statistics suggest that a total of 258 black people were killed by police in the US in 2016.[15]

Such deaths, particularly the killing of Trayvon Martin in 2012, gave voice to the Black Lives Matter movement. 'Rooted in the experiences of Black people in this country who actively resist our dehumanization, #BlackLivesMatter is a call to action and a response to the virulent anti–Black racism that permeates our society'.[16] The movement is based on ideological and political interventions which work to make significant changes in society for black people: '#BlackLivesMatter is working for a world where Black lives are no longer systematically and intentionally targeted for demise. We affirm our contributions to this society, our humanity, and our resilience in the face of deadly oppression'.[17]

Valerie Castile, whose son was the 115th black man to be shot in 2016, said in an interview with CNN about the shooting, "I think he was just black in the wrong place." Her son was stopped for a broken taillight and the video his girlfriend took of the incident shows him reaching for his wallet before he is shot by a white police officer. Valerie Castile made it clear she felt the reason her son was shot was because of his colour: "We're being hunted every day. It's a silent war against African American people as a whole. We're never free." Mildred Haynes, whose son was shot by police in Milwaukee in August 2016, said, "My son is gone due to the police killing my son. I am lost."[18] His death sparked violent protests in Milwaukee, where 40% of the population is African American, resulting in Governor Scott Walker sending in the National Guard. Sadly such reports of young black African American men being killed by the police are commonplace.

Recently in North Carolina, police shot and killed Keith Scott, a black African American male who was told to get out of his car and drop his gun. His wife, Rakeyia Scott, videoed the incident on her phone. An officer is heard shouting, "hands up" with Mrs Scott shouting, "Don't shoot him! He has no weapon! Don't shoot him! He doesn't have a gun he has TBI [traumatic brain injury]." She is then heard shouting, "Keith don't do it" and it is unclear what she is referring to. There are conflicting accounts of the death, with police saying Mr Scott was armed and his family saying he was carrying a book. Officials refused to release body video camera evidence of the shooting. The shooting led to protests on the streets of North Carolina.[19]

More recently, mothers of the movement 'heartbroken mothers' emerged as powerful advocates and supporters of Hillary Clinton in her campaign to become president of the US. She put gun violence and race relations at the centre of her platform in her race to the White House. The women appeared at the Democratic Convention supported by Hilary Clinton in July 2016 to urge Democrats to prioritise criminal justice reform and improve relationships between the police and minority communities. The mothers said they were 'channelling pain into purpose' and 'tragedy into triumph'.[20]

The fragility of race relations in the US has further been affected by the recent spectacular election of Donald J Trump as the 45th President of the United States. Donald John Trump was born in 1946 in New York into a wealthy family. His father Fred Trump was a successful man who owned a large amount of real estate and a number of construction firms. Donald worked for his father and inherited his business in 1971, renaming it the Trump Organization. Since 1971 Donald Trump has assiduously grown both his business and commercial interests and also his reputation as a flamboyant, excessive and straight-talking loudmouth. The skylines of New York and Chicago have both seen his name emblazoned across tall skyscrapers or Trump Towers as well as a multitude of hotels, casinos, golf courses and numerous other property developments in North America, South America, Europe and Asia. He has an estimated net worth of 4.5 billion US dollars and would probably readily admit to having an ego to match.

The 2016 Republican Party presidential primaries were contested by an unwieldy total of 17 candidates, the most candidates ever seen in a presidential primary. Apart from Trump, other nominees included Senator Ted Cruz of Texas, Governor Jeb Bush of Florida, Ben Carson of Maryland and Governor Scott Walker of Wisconsin. One consequence of the overcrowded candidate base was that although all the candidates were positioned in relation to Trump's highly charged rhetorical stance, no single anti-Trump candidate emerged. March 2016 saw Trump securing decisive victories in five 'Super Tuesday' primaries, after which only three candidates remained in contention: Trump, Cruz and John Kasich. Trump managed to score a landslide victory in New York and five other north-eastern states in April, as well as winning the Indiana primary. Cruz suspended his campaign and Trump was declared the Republican nominee by the Republican National Committee chairman on 3 May 2016. Trump passed the threshold of having 1,237 delegates to guarantee his nomination.

Since his victory in November 2016, Trump has used his white privilege and background as a force to mobilise his supporters and the demographic that he supposedly represents. His support remains strongest among white males, with the majority earning less than 50,000 dollars a year and defining themselves as conservative and white non-evangelicals.[21] Trump claims to represent those who vote for him, hardly likely given his wealth, status and privileged background. Trump seized an opportunity – just like the Brexit voters who felt politicians did not speak for them. Trump used his white privilege to claim to understand, and indeed empathise with, white, working class, disenfranchised voters who felt let down, by using issues of immigration, demographic change and the threat of outsiders to mobilise his campaign. Trump used his identity as a white successful businessman to suggest ways in which he could use this to develop strategies while in government. He also used his identity as a political outsider to represent the American people but used his role as someone who is against cultural and demographic changes currently taking place in US society.

Trump's overt attacks on those from minority ethnic communities have legitimised a discourse which encourages racism towards the 'other'. On 16 June 2015 his comments about Mexicans set the tone for this polarising and xenophobic campaign: 'When Mexico sends its people, they're not sending the best. They're not sending you. They're not sending you. They're sending people that have lots of problems, and they're bringing those problems with us. They're bringing drugs. They're bringing crime. They're rapists. And some, I assume are good people'.[22]

First in a written statement and then on 7 December 2015 Donald Trump said he would stop Muslims from entering the US: "Donald J Trump is calling for a total and complete shutdown of Muslims entering the United States until our country's representatives can figure out what is going on."[23] His most recent comments about Khizr Khan and his wife Ghazala Khan on 29 July 2016 were made the day after Khizr Khan spoke at the Democratic National Convention in which he challenged Trump to read the American Constitution. Humayun Khan, the son of Khizr and Ghazala Khan, was a US Muslim army captain who was killed in Iraq in 2004. Donald Trump insinuated in an interview with ABC news that Ghazala Khan had stood silently by her husband while he was on stage because her Muslim religion did not allow her to speak up and voice her opinions. Trump said, "I saw him. He was, you know, very emotional. And probably looked like – a nice guy to me. His wife, if you look at this wife, she was standing there. She had nothing to say. She probably – maybe she wasn't allowed to have anything to say." Later, Ghazala Khan responded that she was too distraught and upset to speak at the event as she could see a large photo of her son displayed behind her at the convention.[24]

Recent polls suggest that four-fifths of Trump supporters say they agree with his plans to build a wall between the US and Mexico to stop immigrants entering the US, to ban Muslims from entering the US and to bar Syrian refugees. There is a suggestion that '… this poll makes clear that Trump triumphed not in spite of his most polarising ideas, but largely because of them'.[25]

Trump's negative xenophobic comments sparked protests resulting in overt violence during his presidential campaign,[26] creating a culture and discourse in which hatred and negativity have become legitimised patterns of behaviour and in which the narrative of whiteness and white identity became privileged at the expense of demonising others. In his attempts to 'Make America Great Again' Donald Trump has created greater divisions, pitting some minority groups against others. Trump's power is part and parcel of his whiteness, which is associated with his privilege, and it is the ownership of this privilege that precludes any other identity.

How whiteness operates in the US

The concept of whiteness refers to a dominant identity in which formations and boundaries of whiteness have specific cultural and economic forms of domination which reinforce the position of privilege. Whiteness, however, is an identity that is historically contingent and can change over time. An understanding of whiteness can reveal how racial practices work. For example, in some instances (such as newspapers, media and TV), a particular type of whiteness is valued – one that is based on a set of white middle-class norms and values in which certain attributes are valued over others (such as appearance and language). While all groups do not occupy a homogeneous position, there are differences in terms of socio-economic background, level of education, accent, dress and language. Despite these differences, the overriding feature is that of whiteness and the privilege associated with it.

A striking example of this is cited by Roediger,[27] who outlines how in the US in the 1920s and 1930s the identity and privilege of whiteness was reinforced to exclude non-whites from buying property and living in certain neighbourhoods due to the offer and availability of selective mortgage packages and specific restrictive housing policies. Consequently, some neighbourhoods used specific measures to stop blacks from buying and living in their neighbourhoods. This process of segregation worked to maintain and keep certain areas as more desirable than others, based on their ethnic population.

Whiteness as property is defined as the privileges conferred upon individual and collective whites through institutional structures and (un)conscious actors. White privilege, which is the expression of whiteness through the maintenance of power, resources, accolades and systems of support through formal and informal structures and procedures, is maintained, and often obscured, through white people's rationalisations in using broad (often racist) categorisations of people of colour and a lack of cultural sensitivity. White privilege manifests itself through people's actions and existing structural procedures, which propagate unequal outcomes for people of colour.[28]

The concept of whiteness in the US (and more recently in the UK) has also been studied in relation to Critical Race Theory, which developed during the 1980s out of the field of legal studies and in which race and racism were taken as central to its analysis. It was seen as an 'oppositional intellectual movement' as it refused to disregard racial inequalities in society.[29] The fundamental principles that underlie Critical Race Theory are: that race and racism are present and indeed endemic in US society and are linked to other forms of oppression such as intersectional identities (gender, class, age and sexuality, among others); a recognition that through the commodification of land and people for profit, whites were able to establish the basis for whiteness as property (as in the Roediger example above). Harris suggests that slavery, '... established and protected an interest in whiteness itself, which shares the critical characteristics of property'.[30] The identity of whiteness gave and indeed guaranteed white people a legal entitlement to freedom in which they remained protected and had a vested interest in protecting their own position within the system. One could argue that this type of system works today, where those who are from white privileged backgrounds use their whiteness to ensure that they maintain and protect their own sense of power and privilege within the hierarchy (which I discuss later in the book).

One of the most important analyses that Critical Race Theory offers is the perspective of 'interest convergence' in which whiteness and white people operate in society to act in their own self-interests, and in which whites will only advance the interests of others (non-whites) when it threatens their own interests and converges with them.[31] Whiteness brings an entitlement to a certain kind of power that blacks do not have; in addition that power comes with certain privileges. The seminal work of Peggy McIntosh is pertinent here and reminds us of the privileges of whiteness. 'White privilege is like an invisible weightless knapsack of special provisions, maps, passports, codebooks, visas, clothes, tools and blank checks'.[32] McIntosh reminds us of the ways in which white privilege works – often to the disadvantage of non-whites. While she recognises that whiteness operates at different levels, she also acknowledges the complexities of it.

> Thinking through unacknowledged male privilege as a phenomenon, I realized that, since hierarchies in our society are interlocking, there was most likely a phenomenon of white privilege that was similarly denied and protected. As a white person, I realized I had been taught about racism as something that puts others at a disadvantage, but had been taught not to see one of its corollary aspects, white privilege, which puts me at an advantage.[33]

She also goes on to acknowledge that

> I think whites are carefully taught not to recognize white privilege, as males are taught not to recognize male privilege. So I have begun in an untutored way to ask what it is like to have white privilege. I have come to see white privilege as an invisible package of unearned assets that I can count on cashing in each day, but about which I was 'meant' to remain oblivious.[34]

Ruth Frankenberg, who wrote about whiteness over 20 years ago, defined it as referring to '... a set of locations that are historically, socially, politically and culturally produced'.[35] Whiteness and white identity are based on a set of social relations in which white people are at the top of a hierarchy by virtue of their white identity and as a result they hold power (consciously or not) over those who are non-white. Whiteness is based on an ideology where white supremacy operates as a given, in which many of those who are white may not necessarily recognise or even acknowledge its existence. Whiteness is based on an identity that is considered to be superior to all other identities. Being white means that goods and resources will be distributed based on white identities occupying a superior position in the hierarchy. There are, however, divisions and hierarchies within the classification of whiteness which create further divisions – these may be based on class, education levels, accent and dress, which further divide white communities. But, the overriding identity will always work as a form of privilege for white groups – over and above that of black or non-white groups.

Sleeter[36] suggests that while identities are socially constructed, they also need to be situated in an objective social location, so one's experiences may be shaped by one's social location but these experiences are also based on one's understanding of identity. 'Thus identifying as white means internalising and using privileges and status associated with white supremacy'.[37]

The history of whiteness and white identity in the US has been analysed within the context of struggles for the control of resources related to power. It has been argued that throughout the 1880s the white working class defined their white identity in opposition to that of blacks because of the competition and fight for jobs, power and status. They did not want to be identified as being powerless and in effect at the bottom of the hierarchy, so were keen to assert their whiteness in order to protect their own position in their fight for jobs and resources.[38] The reinforcing of whiteness as an identity was a process related to the competition of resources. Sleeter suggests that '[w]hite people today in colonialist societies inherit the status and often the property that was (and still is) accumulated within a racialized system, and an identity as white that we take for granted'.[39]

Many white people take their identity for granted in ways that no non-white or black person is able to do. Black people are constantly aware of their identity, particularly in relation to how they are positioned compared with whites. White people are less likely to change systems that benefit and work for them; instead many work hard to protect their own privileges and resist changing systems where they will be disadvantaged. Furthermore, effects and processes of institutional racism will continue to be used by whites as a justification of their superior position in which they hold the keys to power. This in itself works to maintain, reinforce and privilege whiteness and white identity.

Whiteness and education

One example of how whiteness manifests itself is in the classroom. The study of how white identities operate in the classroom has become crucial in how teachers understand not only the identities of their students, but also how their own identities impact on the learning experience. This issue has recently been addressed in classrooms in the US, though to a lesser extent in the UK (education and whiteness is discussed in detail in Chapters Five and Six). Researchers suggest that white teachers must be critical of their own identities in the classroom and examine the impact that their history has had on their own teaching and their opinions of their students.[40] White identity itself should be based on understanding the impact of whiteness. Racism must be a process that is unlearnt and in which historical oppression is understood. Teachers must consider how their teaching can be changed in relation to both of these things. This may be in the form of examining a Eurocentric curriculum and the teaching of black history for an inclusive curriculum.

Some researchers have suggested that there are negative connotations associated with white people accepting their privileged identity – these may be related to feelings of 'depression, helplessness and anxiety',[41] which are needed for the development of a critical perspective on race relations in the US. While some white people do feel guilty because of the past actions of their ancestors, they still benefit from their own identity of whiteness – whether they like it or not! A colour-blind approach adopted in the US is one way in which race issues have been addressed, however Sleeter suggests that '[p]eople do not deny seeing what they actually do not see. Rather, they profess to be colour blind when trying to suppress negative images they attach to people of colour'.[42] So, a colour-blind approach masks real negative images that white people have of black people based on negative stereotypes. 'Examining the ways in which White racism manifests itself in whites and, consequently, affects children of colour can lead to denials as well as cautionary explanations as to why these beliefs are actually "true" rather than racist'.[43]

Quite often white people – and white teachers – respond to discussions of whiteness, white privilege and racism in a defensive manner. This has been found in relation to affirmative action programmes, which many whites feel give special privileges to people of colour. There is evidence to suggest that many white students, for example, feel that affirmative action is a positive initiative, as long as it does not disadvantage them by preventing them from attending the best schools and universities.[44] Many scholars have suggested that there are justifications for affirmative action in higher education admissions, particularly in relation to historical discrimination which disadvantages blacks.[45] There is also evidence to suggest that many white people do not see the disadvantages that black people face due to racism and often dismiss those disadvantages as being attributed to racism – this in itself can be seen as a covert or unconscious form of racism. McIntyre[46] calls this 'White talk'. White talk is a negative strategy used by white people to circumvent their own role in perpetuating racism. Quite often this is based on relying on popular stereotypes of black people related to deficit and negative thinking about the lives of black people. Part of this stems from justifying their own racism and the belief that whites are superior to blacks. This is based on an unquestioned and uncritical view of themselves as white people. White people see themselves and other white people as being worthy – a rhetoric related to Peggy McIntosh's 'knapsack of privileges' – in that they are conformist, law-abiding citizens. This is in comparison to black people, who are seen as disadvantaged, dangerous and untrustworthy

– and *not* worthy. In some respects this may take place on an unconscious level in which whites are unaware how their own beliefs affect their interactions with blacks, but in many cases this happens on a conscious level and whites overtly use their white identity as a form of privilege and entitlement – particularly in relation to competition for jobs and prestige (see Chapter Eight on the labour market). In this process, white people perpetuate their own white racism in white spaces and white-dominated environments. The stereotypes and deficit thinking that some white people employ when thinking of black people inevitably affect their views of minority groups and this in turn works to disadvantage those from non-white backgrounds. Some white people are clearly aware of their sense of power and privilege, others less so. White people are able to move within their own white culture of power but it is important that they are able to recognise their own privilege and the advantages that their own privilege brings. As Riggins suggests, an important way in which racism manifests itself happens covertly, '... conveyed primarily through subtleties of face to face interaction such as hostile staring, silence, joking and labelling'.[47]

Others have suggested that white privilege has maintained its dominance in more covert, institutional ways that can appear to be non-racial and non-racist.[48] A new racism has emerged in which appropriate racial discourse and language is used and is acceptable. Bonilla-Silva and Forman suggest that there has been a re-articulation of dominant racial themes (less overt expressions of racism but more resentment based on policies such as affirmative action and welfare). This has in turn resulted in a new way of talking about racism and racial issues in public places which they call a new *racetalk*. They suggest that '[t]he new racial ideology continues to help in the reproduction of white supremacy'.[49] There is a suggestion here that even though whites know that they should not display racist attitudes towards blacks, the advantages that blacks have – such as affirmative action – mean that some white people themselves feel hard done by. However, while many white people oppose affirmative action, there is evidence to suggest that rather than black African Americans benefitting from affirmative action, the main beneficiaries have been white women.[50]

In this sense, Bonilla-Silva and Forman suggest that

> the liberal, free market and pragmatic rhetoric of colour-blind racism allows whites to defend white supremacy in an apparently non-racial manner. Colour-blind racism allows whites to appear 'not racist', preserve their privileged status, blame blacks for their lower status and criticise any institutional approach – such as affirmative action – that attempts to ameliorate racial inequality.[51]

In this sense, white people who use a colour-blind approach and rationale do so to protect and defend their own white privilege. Whiteness is associated with historical privilege and power, which continue to benefit whites regardless of their class (although it may work differently for white working- and middle-class groups) and other intersectional identities. Whiteness is not just an individual identity, it is one that is embedded in different institutions – such as schools, universities and the media – as being *the* predominant identity. In such white spaces, whiteness and white Western practices are the norm and those which do not comply with these are seen as outsiders and others. The white practices and identity of whiteness are afforded a certain type of privilege that dominates all others, in which the privileges associated with whiteness are only available to white groups who operate in these spaces – often at the expense of non-white groups. Some black scholars have argued that the supremacist ideology of whiteness has been used to suppress black people and their thinking,[52] others have suggested that in order to understand how whiteness operates, it must be understood from an anti-racist and equity struggle perspective.[53]

Understanding white identity in the UK

In the UK, identities of whiteness have been understood differently compared with the US and it is only recently that the concept of whiteness has been given much attention. There is relatively little research which has explored the concept in the same depth as it has been explored in the US. Early work by Bonnett[54] suggests that the identity of whiteness was not used to identify the white working class until after imperialism. This group were seen as being on the boundaries and margins of whiteness and seen as an 'in between people'.[55]

At the end of the 1980s whiteness as an identity was under threat due to the end of the Keynesian era. Preston suggests '[t]he new Thatcher government was prepared to use moral panics about immigration, crime and the idle working class, with the support of the ascendant "new" middle classes, to introduce a number of authoritarian, imperialist and pro-market policies'.[56] At this time, the white working class were seen as 'scroungers', living off the dole, not wanting to work, lawless and fearful.[57] Garner identifies whiteness as '... a paradigm, a way of understanding the social world' in which 'white is a position of relative privilege, albeit highly uneven, contingent and situational'.[58]

Scholars in the UK have also begun to use Critical Race Theory as a basis for understanding how whiteness and white privilege operate, particularly in relation to the educational experiences of minority groups. The influential and ground-breaking work of David Gillborn, the leading scholar on Critical Race Theory in the UK, is based on an analysis of educational policy making and its failings in relation to the experiences of minority groups. He suggests that 'Critical race theory promotes a different perspective on white supremacy than the limited and extreme understandings usually denoted by the term in everyday language'.[59] Gillborn uses an intersectional analysis to explore how whiteness operates for different groups – those from middle- and working-class backgrounds. He suggests that the white working class are beneficiaries of whiteness, but '... are also at times in a liminal position, where they can be demonised when necessary or useful ... they provide a buffer, a safety zone that protects the white middle classes'.[60]

Conclusions

In this chapter I have discussed how whiteness and white identities operate as a form of privilege in society. White privilege can operate in subtle, nuanced ways, for example when someone pushes in front of a black person in the queue or when a black person is stopped at customs. In these examples, white privilege allows white identities to be seen as superior, which manifests in the overt treatment of blacks as less important and inferior. I suggest that in order to understand the discourse of what it means to be white, this must be understood in two different political and social contexts, that of the UK and that of the US. While class is clearly important in the narratives of acceptable and non-acceptable forms of whiteness, I argue that the identity of *being white* – regardless of class – takes precedence over all other forms of identity. Intersectional identities come to the fore after whiteness makes it mark, the identity of whiteness is however, the first determinant of how groups are positioned, followed by other markers such as class, gender, religion, age and sexuality, among others. I am not suggesting that class does not play a part in the positioning of groups in society, I am merely suggesting that its intersection with whiteness produces a different discourse from which judgements about individuals are made.

This chapter has argued that whiteness and white privilege dominate all aspects of society and suggests that those from non-white backgrounds, because of their identity, are positioned as inferior to whites in a society in which white identities predominate. Historical dimensions and understandings of whiteness in the US stem from the history of slavery and the dominant construction of whiteness as the norm, in which black identity is seen as the 'other'. Such identities manifest to position black identity as inferior and white identity as superior, in which an historical understanding of white master and black slave reinforces the privilege of whiteness. In the UK, understandings of whiteness stem from processes of structural racism which work to disadvantage blacks and advantage whites. This is also based on a denial of the processes of structural and institutional racism that manifest in different ways (for example through education, the labour market, health and poverty). Such discourses further work to perpetuate the myth that racism is no longer a problem and has been dealt with.

In the following chapter, I explore how a *particular* kind of whiteness is valued in which those from Gypsy and Traveller backgrounds, by virtue of their white identity, do not possess the privileges of whiteness. I suggest that Gypsy and Traveller groups are positioned as outsiders in a society which values a certain kind of *acceptable* whiteness.

THREE

Not white enough

In the previous chapter I discussed the ways in which whiteness and white identity work as a form of privilege in which whiteness is protected at the expense of others (notably those from black and minority ethnic backgrounds). While the main argument of this book is the notion that whiteness and white identity are manifested by protecting the status quo at the same time as maintaining the predominant position of white people, in this chapter I suggest that a particular kind of whiteness is privileged and protected, which I refer to as acceptable and non-acceptable forms of whiteness. Acceptable forms of whiteness are based on the perception of conforming to society's expectations (for example paying taxes and being a good citizen). This form of acceptable whiteness is often applied to those from middle-class backgrounds in which other forms of hierarchies based on language, dress, education and taste distinguish one group from another. An example of non-acceptable whiteness is seen in the use of the word 'chav', a derogatory term used to describe those from white working-class backgrounds who have a penchant for designer clothing such as Burberry. The discourse that emerges around the use of the word 'chav' is based on describing those from working-class backgrounds as being uncouth, unworthy and unkempt. It is used as an offensive and derogatory term to demonise those from poor, white, working-class backgrounds.

In this chapter I argue that different shades of whiteness are related to non-acceptable forms of whiteness. I refer to unacceptable or illegitimate forms of whiteness to explain the position and experiences of Gypsy and Traveller groups who live in the UK. I suggest that the whiteness attributed to Gypsies and

Travellers is a form of *non-acceptable* whiteness, which does not have the same status or privilege accorded to those from white middle-class backgrounds. I suggest that while many Gypsies and Travellers have a white ethnic identity, they do not have access to the same advantages associated with acceptable forms of whiteness (such as being seen as paying taxes, which equates to being a law-abiding citizen).

This chapter will begin by providing a contextual background of Gypsy and Traveller groups in the UK and Europe. It will argue that in all areas of society, Gypsy and Traveller groups remain positioned on the margins and periphery; they are disadvantaged in education, employment, housing and mental health. The chapter will conclude by drawing on a case study to examine how Gypsy and Traveller parents and their children are treated in schools due to their undesirable identity of whiteness.

Gypsies and Travellers in the UK

Definitions

There is linguistic evidence to suggest that Gypsies and Travellers originated from Northern India over 1,000 years ago.[1] It is thought that they arrived in England around the reign of Henry VIII. They were originally thought to have originated from Egypt, hence the name given to them as 'Egyptians'. This changed from 'Gyptians' and then later on to 'Gypsies'. Many Gypsy and Traveller groups spoke the Romany language, which has its roots in the Indian Hindi language. Today, a large number of Gypsy and Traveller families are keen to teach their children Romany and consequently many are bilingual and speak Romany at home.

Gypsy and Traveller groups include those from a diverse range of communities such as English Romany Gypsies, Irish, Scottish and Welsh Travellers, Bargees (those living on barges or boats) and Travelling Showmen (fairground and circus families). More recently, there has been an increase in New Age Travellers, who tend to be individuals who do not have ethnic roots from the Gypsy and Traveller community but have decided to choose to opt out of society and lead a nomadic and travelling lifestyle.

They do not necessarily identify with the cultural mores attributed to Gypsy and Traveller communities.

Characteristics of Gypsies and Travellers in the UK

The Equality Act[2] introduced in 2010 is an important piece of legislation for the inclusion of Gypsy and Traveller groups in which they are recognised as an ethnic group. The Equality Act brings together all previous legislation into one single Act which provides a legal framework to protect the rights of individuals to advance equality of opportunity. The Equality Act also contains 'protected characteristics', which include race. The Act states that Romany Gypsies and Irish Travellers are classified as ethnic groups and hence are protected under the Equality Act.

In 2011 for the first time the census included a question dedicated to the ethnic group Gypsy or Irish Traveller.[3] The census box was not intended for those from European Roma backgrounds as these groups have distinct and very different identities to those from UK Gypsy and Irish Traveller backgrounds.

According to the last census in 2011, a total of 58,000 individuals (0.1% of the population of England and Wales) identified themselves as Gypsy or Irish Traveller, which is the classification given on the census. The majority of individuals who identified as being from this group were more likely to say they had an English national identity (66%) and that they were Christian (64%). Gypsy or Irish Travellers were the group in the census who had the highest proportion of any ethnic group with no academic or professional qualifications (60%) – which is three times higher than England and Wales as a whole (23%). The older the Gypsy or Irish Traveller, the more likely they were to have no qualifications. They were also more likely to have the lowest proportion of individuals who were economically active (47%) compared with 63% for England and Wales as a whole. The most common reason for Gypsy or Irish Travellers not working was looking after the family or the home. They were also more likely than any other ethnic group to be self-employed (26% compared with 14% for England and Wales as a whole) and more likely to have dependent children (45% compared with 29% for England and Wales as a whole).[4]

The census data suggests that those who identify as Gypsy or Irish Traveller are one of the most disadvantaged of all ethnic groups. They were more than twice as likely as the overall population to live in social housing (41% compared with 16%) and were less likely to own their own homes (21% compared with 26%). They were also more likely than any other ethnic group to suffer from poor health; they had the lowest proportion of individuals who said their health was 'good' or 'very good' compared with 81% of the overall population. Of those who lived in a caravan or other temporary structure, 70% said their health was 'good' or 'very good', and those who lived in a house or bungalow were slightly more likely to say they had 'good' or 'very good' health (72%).[5]

Experiences of Gypsy and Travellers in society

Gypsy and Traveller groups have the lowest levels of educational attainment of any ethnic group. In their early years, they are less likely to develop as well as other children, which has a significant impact on future development.[6] Recent evidence shows that in 2013/14 only 13.8% of Gypsy/Roma children achieved at least five A*–C GCSEs and 17.5% of Traveller children compared with 60.3% of other white children. Gypsy, Roma and Traveller children also have high rates of permanent and fixed-term exclusions compared with other groups, which is also the case for black Caribbean and mixed/white ethnic groups.[7] Gypsy and Traveller groups are also less likely to make the transition into higher education.[8]

Gypsy and Traveller groups experience greater accommodation problems compared with other ethnic groups. According to the Department for Communities and Local Government (DCLG) in January 2016, there were a total of 21,306 caravan sites in England, of which 7,046 (33%) were on socially rented sites, 11,454 (54%) on privately rented sites and 13% on unauthorised sites.[9] The lack of authorised sites makes it difficult for families to settle in one place for long periods of time, leaving them with no choice but to move from one unauthorised site to another. The

United Nations Human Rights Council (UNHRC)[10] has argued that lack of adequate accommodation is a critical issue for Gypsy and Traveller groups in England and can have devastating effects on the lives of individuals in terms of health, poverty and access to employment. In 2011 the Committee on the Elimination of Racial Discrimination (CERD) recommended the importance of providing adequate accommodation to meet the needs of Gypsy and Traveller groups in England (including transit sites).[11]

Gypsy and Traveller groups are also likely to suffer poor health compared with other ethnic groups, and have poorer access to healthcare and primary care.[12] They are also more likely to suffer poorer mental health compared with other ethnic groups. The EHRC quotes research carried out by the DCLG, which states:

> A progress report by the Department of Communities and Local Government in 2012 noted the problems experienced by Gypsies and Travellers compared with the general population; lower life expectancy, high infant mortality rates, high maternal mortality rates, low child immunisation levels, higher prevalence of anxiety and depression, chronic cough or bronchitis (even after smoking is taken into account), asthma, chest pain and diabetes.[13]

Gypsies and Travellers have poor access to general practitioners (GPs) and primary care and are less likely to be registered with a GP and report discrimination when accessing healthcare. Many Gypsies and Travellers are not registered with a GP and report a lack of cultural awareness, being seen as 'problematic' patients as reasons for their experiences with healthcare professionals.[14]

The numbers of Gypsies, Roma and Travellers in prison is high compared with their representation in the general population. In 2013/14, 4% of this group were in prison compared with 0.1% in the 2011 census population.[15] Gypsy and Traveller groups in prison also report being unsafe, victims of violence, bullying and racism, and are more likely than other groups to be at risk of suicide.[16]

Gypsy and Traveller groups are less likely to occupy senior decision-making roles in the labour market (such as in the police service, law and the judiciary). The EHRC states, '[i]n Britain, only two councillors are known to have a Gypsy or Traveller background'.[17] Negative images of Gypsies and Travellers are perpetrated by the biased, racist and negative stereotyping of these groups in the media.

Media portrayals of Gypsies and Travellers in the UK

The evidence above suggests that Gypsy and Traveller groups remain one of the most disadvantaged groups in the UK. There is also evidence to suggest that they experience overt racism. One of the ways in which this racism is legitimised is through the stereotypical images associated with Gypsies and Travellers portrayed in the media. Media images are often based on tales of Gypsies and Travellers as being dirty, thieves, aggressive, violent and untrusting. A slight shift in this stereotype was evident in the recent documentary *My Big Fat Gypsy Wedding*, which portrays Gypsy and Traveller groups as having lavish lifestyles typified by extravagant and ostentatious weddings. Gypsies and Travellers are portrayed as lacking 'taste' when compared with the behaviours of the general population. Two different opposing images of Gypsies and Travellers are presented by the media: one of an underclass that do not abide by the laws of the land and are not 'good citizens' and the other of extravagance associated with bad taste and overindulgence. Such images not only fuel racism and xenophobia towards these groups, they also demonstrate how a certain kind of whiteness is accepted in society. This whiteness associated with Gypsies and Travellers is an unacceptable form of whiteness. Gypsies and Travellers are demonised for not wanting to live alongside non-Gypsy communities, for keeping their distance and only 'mixing with their own' and being outsiders. For many Gypsies and Travellers, leaving their own communities and living with 'gaugos' (non-Gypsies) is a huge risk, one which many are not prepared to take.

Media coverage and programmes such as *My Big Fat Gypsy Wedding* have been shown to increase levels of racism and prejudice towards Gypsy and Traveller groups in the UK. After Channel 4's controversial poster campaign which read 'Bigger, Fatter, Gypsier',[18] the London Travellers' Unit complained about the use of the word 'gypsier' for conveying racist overtones and also about stereotypical images used in the campaign. This is just one example among many others of the media portraying overt racist, negative stereotypes of Gypsies and Travellers, which are used to demonise and perpetuate images of them as groups who deserve to be racially abused.

Gypsy and Traveller groups in Europe

The nomenclature of nomadic groups in Europe is different to that of the UK. Generally, the term Roma is used in the EU (particularly in policy documents) and refers to individuals who are from various ethnicities such as Roma, Gypsies, Travellers and other groups such as Manouches, Ashkali, Sinti and Boyash. The EU estimates that of the 10–12 million who live in the whole of Europe, 6 million live in the EU.

In 2010 the EU Commission outlined their Communication on the economic and social integration of the Roma in Europe, in which they stressed that it is the role of all European nations to have a joint responsibility for the integration of Roma in society and to improve conditions for these groups. They recognise the poor social and economic conditions faced by the Roma and suggest ways forward to address these. 'The discrimination, social exclusion and segregation which Roma face are mutually reinforcing. They face limited access to high quality education, difficulties in integration into the labour market, correspondingly low level incomes, and poor health which in turn results in higher mortality rates and lower life expectancy compared with non-Roma'.[19] The Communication policy outlines the effect of how Roma groups are treated in society: 'Roma exclusion entails not only significant direct costs for public budgets [but also] ... indirect costs through losses in productivity'.[20]

Following this consultation document in 2011, the EU adopted the national strategy for Roma integration for addressing and dealing with policies and measures to be taken by each EU country.

The commission asks the EU institutions to endorse this EU Framework for National Roma Integration

Strategies. It is a means to complement and reinforce the EU's equality legislation and policies by addressing, at national, regional and local level, but also through dialogue with and participation of the Roma, the specific needs of Roma regarding equal access to employment, education, housing and healthcare.[21]

In 2015, the EU published a report on the implementation of an EU Framework for National Roma Integration, which shows some improvements in the lives of Roma. It stated that '[t]ranslating national strategies into action at local level is in an early phase and needs to be supported with sustainable funding, capacity building and full involvement of local authorities and civil society, and robust monitoring to bring about the much-needed tangible impact at local level, where challenges arise'.[22]

There is a great deal of evidence to demonstrate the prejudice and inequalities faced by Roma groups in Europe. Such evidence points to anti-Gypsy stereotypes in the media, a lack of recognition of Roma history and overt racism against Roma groups across Europe. Roma groups are disadvantaged by their education, have poor access to housing and employment, and suffer from mental and physical health problems.

In the following section I use education as an example to demonstrate how Gypsies and Travellers in the UK continue to experience racism, discrimination and marginalisation in schools.

Education of Gypsies and Travellers in the UK

Policy context

There are no national policies for the inclusion of Gypsy and Traveller groups in the UK on education, though there are more generic policies on the inclusion of minority ethnic groups and education. Scotland, Northern Ireland and Wales have their own individual policies regarding the inclusion of Gypsy and Traveller children. However, Gypsy and Traveller children are (like all other children) protected under the United Nations Convention on the Rights of the Child. Under Articles 28 and 29 all children have the right to an education. Articles 12 to 15 specifically state that children have the right to express their opinions and have the right to obtain information to express those views. Article 29 is even more explicit and states: 'Education should be directed at developing the child's personality and talents; preparing the child for active life as an adult; fostering respect for basic human rights; developing respect for the child's own cultural and national values and those of others; and developing respect for the natural environment'.[23] The question I want to pose is: Do Gypsy and Traveller children receive these benefits? Benefits that they are rightfully entitled to? Much of the research seems to suggest not entirely, certainly not compared with other children who may be gaining more from their educational experiences. As discussed in this chapter, many Gypsy and Traveller families and their children feel excluded and dissatisfied with their educational experiences, and certainly feel marginalised when they disclose their identity.

As a result of the publication of *Education for Citizenship and the teaching of democracy in schools*,[24] schools were required to include the teaching of citizenship as part of the national curriculum. Initially, there was little reference to human rights or race equality in the report, but subsequent curriculum guidance did include a reference to a human rights agenda in relation to the teaching of citizenship in schools.[25] While there was an emphasis on the teaching of citizenship to include a human rights and inclusive agenda, this has not been borne out in the real experiences of many minority ethnic groups – particularly those of Gypsies and Travellers for whom schools and the structure of education are not responsive to their needs. If the curriculum was inclusive of the cultures of Gypsy and Traveller groups, parents would feel that their cultures were valued and respected and understood by majority communities.[26]

School attendance

All parents are legally expected to send their children to school. If they do not, they can be prosecuted. If parents do not provide schools with a valid reason for non-attendance, schools can provide parents with a parenting order, an education supervision order, a school attendance order or a fine (penalty notice). The parenting order requires parents to attend parenting classes whereas an education supervision order requires parents to have appointed a supervisor to enable them to get their child to attend school. A school attendance order requires parents to send their child to a school within a certain time and if they do not they will be prosecuted. A penalty notice includes a fine and possible prosecution (which may include a jail sentence of up to three months).[27]

Gypsy and Traveller children are exempt from these provisions if they can prove that their family is engaged in a business that means they have to travel; if the child has attended regularly while the family has been engaged in the business; and if the child has attended for at least 200 half days during the previous school year.[28] While this clearly demonstrates some flexibility for those from Gypsy and Traveller backgrounds, other families may see this as an excuse for Gypsies and Travellers not having to send their children to school on a regular basis.

Funding for Gypsy and Traveller children

The Ethnic Minority Achievement Grant (EMAG) was allocated from the Standards Fund by the Department for Education and Science (DES) in 1999 to replace section 11 grants made to local authorities. The grant was set up to meet the needs of minority ethnic pupils, including those who had English as an additional language. The grant was used to fund ways to increase the standards of achievement for those from different minority ethnic groups, particularly groups who were at greater risk of underachievement. The funding of Traveller Education Services fell under the EMAG. At the time, the grant was paid directly to schools and was used to cover costs of relevant activities (including salaries) which would contribute to raising the achievement of minority ethnic groups who were at risk of underachievement. Funding was allocated to schools based on the number of minority ethnic pupils attending. In 2010 the funding that was ring-fenced for EMAG in England was £204 million, but in 2011 the EMAG was abandoned as a specific individual grant to support the underachievement of minority ethnic pupils. However, in England, as a result of the Coalition Government's cuts to funding in 2010, EMAG was one of the first to take a hit. Consequently, EMAG is no longer a separate ring-fenced grant to support the educational achievement of minority ethnic pupils. This is one example of the Coalition Government's stance on inclusive policy making which failed to address inequality, equity and social justice. Those at risk and those who were the most marginalised were hit hardest by education cuts. This also included funding for Traveller Education Services. Funding that was previously under the EMAG remit was dissolved as part of the general schools' budget. As a result, the funding was used for any other support at the discretion of the head teacher.

The Traveller Education Service, which was funded under EMAG, has been a very important service for Gypsy and Traveller families. Many Gypsy and Traveller families have relied heavily on the support of the Traveller Education Service, often seeing them as the link between their communities and the school, and sometimes providing isolated Gypsy and Traveller families with a lifeline to other families and communities. The Traveller Education Service works to support the needs of families who are either permanently resident or nomadic and to facilitate and support Gypsy and Traveller pupils in their school experience. A key function of the service has been to raise awareness of Gypsy and Traveller culture within schools to foster an inclusive ethos and to support Gypsy and Traveller parents in helping them to raise the attendance and achievement of their children. The Traveller Education Service also contributes to in-service training to break down stereotypes of Gypsy and Traveller groups and to share good practice regarding the teaching and support of Gypsy and Traveller pupils and communities. Many schools use the service to provide teaching materials and resources which can support the inclusion of Gypsy and Traveller pupils in schools. There is evidence to suggest that Gypsy and Traveller communities feel that the Traveller Education Service is valued and provides them with important support that affects how they communicate with schools and whether they decide to send their children to school.[29] The lack of funding for Traveller Education

Services means many Gypsy and Traveller children will be at risk of receiving little or no education at all.

There is recent evidence to suggest that approximately one third of local authorities have not identified support for Gypsy and Traveller pupils and their families, and where the service does exist there have been severe cuts in staff numbers in which Traveller Education Service workers have their roles restricted or moved to other areas.[30] Because funding has shifted to the pupil premium, this means local authorities can decide how to spend their money. As a result, the lack of funding to provide support for Gypsy and Traveller pupils has either fallen dramatically or does not exist at all. The Irish Traveller Movement in Britain has outlined the importance of continued financial support for Traveller Education Services in England. They suggest that the services:

> have been recognised by the European Commission as a model of good practice in engaging with the education needs of Gypsy, Roma and Traveller communities. The government should closely monitor the impact of financial restraint on Traveller Education Support Services to ensure that the impact of local authority cuts does not fall disproportionately on these educationally vulnerable racial groups.[31]

They also go on to argue that under the obligations of the 2011 EU Framework for National Roma Integration Strategies, the government should think about setting specific targets to improve the educational achievement of these disadvantaged groups.

School experiences

There is a plethora of evidence to suggest that Gypsy and Traveller children experience overt racism, exclusion and marginalisation in schools, both from their peers and from their teachers;[32] there is also a lack of understanding about what constitutes a suitable education for the needs of Gypsy and Traveller groups.

There is also evidence to suggest that even when schools have inclusive policies, they do not necessarily have good practice measures in place, for example many Gypsy and Traveller children continue to report experiences of racism, bullying and exclusion from their peers. What is needed is a much more coherent approach adopted by schools so that schools have detailed guidance which is followed, rather than a tick box exercise. This is also related to a strong leadership ethos in which schools must have leaders who take issues of social justice and equity seriously in their quest to ensure that all children have positive experiences in the school environment, regardless of their ethnic background. In order for effective learning to take place, children must feel valued and accepted in an environment in which they are able to be proud of their backgrounds, identity and culture. Inclusivity must take place at all levels. For many Gypsy and Traveller children, their learning traditionally takes place in the home environment and families continue to emphasise the skills their children learn from watching, copying and working alongside their families in a community environment. In order for parents to be confident to send their children to school, the school must be seen as a safe and secure place. Many Gypsy and Traveller families and their children feel excluded from society and schools as they do not feel their needs are recognised or addressed. They also feel that the racism and discrimination they experience reflect the general lack of understanding within society about their culture and lifestyle. Despite the government's rhetoric on an inclusive and citizenship policy agenda in schools, Gypsy and Traveller children continue to be excluded and marginalised.[33]

While some schools make an effort to understand Gypsy and Traveller families and their children's educational needs, others are failing in their efforts. A lack of understanding on the part of schools about the learning environment for Gypsy and Traveller children is often apparent. Engaging in education is defined as structured learning: attending school at certain times, dedicated time to certain subjects, structured homework and passing exams. These processes enable young people to make successful transitions into further or higher education or the labour market. However, this system does not allow for deviations from this structured learning. It does not account for learning taking place in the home environment. Many Gypsy and Traveller parents do not feel that schools are able to provide their children with the education that is suited to their needs or address their cultural mores. For many Gypsy and Traveller parents, education (or learning and instruction) takes place in the home environment and parents feel that schools and their physical spaces do not necessarily provide their children with a safe environment that is conducive to learning. Furthermore, Gypsy and Traveller parents want their children to learn the specific skills that are needed in order to be part of their community. Addressing the needs of Gypsy and Traveller children would be more effective if schools could accommodate the practicalities of Gypsy family life within a more flexible curriculum.

Many Gypsy and Traveller parents are often afraid to make complaints for fear of not being taken seriously and when their children experience name calling or racism in schools, this is often unrecognised by teachers. When they do complain, Gypsy and Traveller children are often portrayed as the villains in such instances. They are labelled as the 'aggressor' or 'troublemaker' or 'cause of the problem' rather than the 'victim'. Gypsy and Traveller parents report that their children are taught to 'stick up for themselves', a trait that is often interpreted as 'trouble making' and perpetuating further aggression. Consequently, name calling, racism and bullying results in Gypsy and Traveller parents wanting to withdraw their children from school altogether or choose alternative forms of education (such as home schooling).[34]

In many cases, when parents have complained about bullying and racism, schools often fail to use anti-bullying and anti-racism policies and procedures to respond to or investigate such incidents. Stereotypical images in the media and in society more generally portray Gypsy and Traveller groups as rule breakers and troublemakers, hence when they do make complaints to schools these are either not believed or indeed not dealt with effectively.[35]

All schools are expected to have anti-racist and anti-bullying policies in place, however there is evidence to suggest that the mere presence of these policies does not suggest that the rights of some groups – such as Gypsies and Travellers – are protected, particularly in relation to the obligation of schools to foster and promote social inclusion and social justice for the education of *all* children.[36]

In the following sections I draw on a case study to demonstrate how the whiteness associated with being a Gypsy and Traveller is an unacceptable form of whiteness in the UK.

THE SMITH FAMILY

The Smith family live on a privately owned site on the south coast of England. The Smiths are a relatively affluent family. They define themselves as English Gypsies. The Smiths have been living on their privately owned site for over 30 years and they live with other extended family members. The site itself is located in a semi-rural village just on the outskirts of a small town. The village is an affluent middle-class community, employment is high and the majority of the residents own their own homes and a car. The village presents a picture of a rural idyll: it is clean and surrounded by quiet country roads, green fields and several ponds. The village itself is relatively small, consisting of a village hall, a primary school, a doctor's surgery, a dentist and a row of local shops to serve the community. The site is set back from the main road along a secluded dirt track. The site is clean, well kept and very orderly.

Mr and Mrs Smith have one daughter Amy, aged 14, and one son Johnny, aged 16. The Smiths had decided to take Amy out of school and home-educate her because she was experiencing bullying from the other students and also felt she was being discriminated against by two of the teachers. Mr and Mrs Smith both wanted to be part of the interview and so were interviewed together, with Amy. They described their daughter's experience:

'At first Amy was fine, she was struggling with the learning but she was getting on with it and didn't really say much about being a Traveller, she thought it was best not to say anything. But then she spoke about it and started to get some abuse from the other kids. She would get upset and was scared to tell us about it and we went up the school.'

Mrs Smith described how she felt that as soon as the teachers saw them, they were afraid they were going to cause trouble.

'We didn't go up there shouting and screaming, why would we do that? We went up there and said it has to stop. We didn't say what has happened and this and that, we just said we want those kids to stop calling our daughter those names, like gypo, pikey and that she stinks. The head teacher said they need to look into it, we knew they wouldn't do anything about it, so we took her out.'

Mr and Mrs Smith felt that there were other incidents that Amy would talk about at the school where she was being treated differently by the teachers because she was a Traveller. One example included Amy refusing to do physical education lessons because her parents did not want her to participate in these lessons, but the school were not very understanding about this.

'They didn't take any opportunity to talk to us about why we don't want her to do it, they just went ahead and said something like, and we can't give you special treatment or nothing. But we weren't asking for any kind of special treatment from them, we just wanted them to understand our side.'

Mr and Mrs Smith spoke a great deal about the way they were treated by others and also how their children were treated because of their identity. When discussing the bullying their daughter had experienced, Mr Smith said it was the other white children who tended to display the worst type of behaviour.

'It was mainly the other white kids who were the worst offenders, they were the ones who called Amy all the names. The black kids didn't because they know what it's like to be called racist names themselves. We don't have anything to do with the blacks but they have to do the same thing. Stick up for themselves. They know what we know. In this country, we are the blacks. We're lower than the blacks, nobody has a good word to say about us.'

Mr and Mrs Smith's views on the racist name calling was interesting; the white children who called Amy racist names were from working-class backgrounds and according to the Smiths they lived in social housing.

> 'We get picked on because we are Gypsies, and they think we don't work or do anything else. But we do work, a lot of those kids I want to know if their parents are working like we are? They are the ones who live in the council homes. They don't go to work like we do, instead they stay at home and get benefits but we're not like that. We work for a living.'

Mr Smith felt that his family was judged differently to those from white working-class backgrounds who may or may not have been claiming state benefits, but who lived in social housing. While on the one hand Mr Smith felt the type of racism he was experiencing was similar (in some respects) to that of black families, on the other hand he emphasised it was due to his Gypsy identity.

> 'If there was another family who was a well to do family and they spoke in a certain way, they would be treated differently to us. We get treated this way because we are Gypsies, those people who live in the council estates they don't get treated like us. They are treated better than us, we seem to be the worst of the lot.'

Mr Smith felt that Gypsies were treated in a certain way because of the stereotypes that were portrayed about them in the media.

> 'People see us a certain way and treat us like that, we are the lowest group in the pile because we are Gypsies. There are other white groups who are not treated like we are, there are stereotypes out there about us and they are believed about Gypsies and Travellers. Everyone thinks we're dirty, that we leave rubbish in every place we visit, yes that happens, but that's not all of us. There are good and bad apples and the newspapers and media always pick on the bad ones.'

The Smiths spoke about many instances in which they had experienced overt racism from the police and other agencies. They felt this was specifically because of their Gypsy identity.

'We are seen as white because we are not black, we are not seen in the same ways as black people and so when we experience racism, it's not understood as racism. But we are also not seen in the same ways as other whites. Those white people who are posh and maybe professionals would never see us like them and those ones who are more like us if you think – their backgrounds – the more working class ones, they don't see us like them either. It's as if we're white but we're not really because we're not treated like we are white. Lots of people in society and in the world, don't understand anything about our culture and what we stand for.'

Conclusions

It was noted in 2003 by the DES that Gypsy and Traveller pupils remain 'the group most at risk in the education system'.[37] Fourteen years on, this is still the case but in some respects one could argue that the situation has deteriorated as Gypsies and Travellers are more likely than any other ethnic group to have lower levels of educational qualifications or be unemployed and are at most risk of mental health problems.[38] Many commentators fail to examine the marginalisation faced by Gypsy and Traveller groups. Stereotypes of Gypsies and Travellers as being dirty, thieving and untrustworthy are linked to stereotypes of Gypsies and Travellers not wanting to send their children to school. Gypsy and Traveller parents want their children to go to school and receive an education, but with the expectation that schools can ensure that their children will be looked after and that they can provide a secure, safe and non-threatening environment in which learning can take place.[39]

Severe cuts in funding for agencies, such as the Traveller Education Service which supports the needs of Gypsy and Traveller children, are a demonstration of the further marginalisation and exclusion of a group already marginalised. Gypsy and Traveller groups represent an *unacceptable* form of whiteness that is not worthy of recognition or support. In a society which values a certain shade of whiteness, Gypsy and Traveller groups will continue to represent an unacceptable shade of whiteness, a group whose needs are rarely recognised or addressed.

FOUR

Intersectionality: gender, race and class

This chapter will explore how intersectionality – identities of gender, race and class – operate to exclude and privilege certain groups. The chapter will argue that class and gender play a key role in the positioning of black and minority ethnic groups in society and discuss the experiences of black and Asian groups in relation to how stereotypes operate to marginalise and exclude certain groups. While I argue in this book that whiteness and white identities operate as a form of privilege in society to maintain and perpetuate the position of white elites, I also suggest that a certain type of whiteness advantages some over others. Intersecting and competing identities – particularly class – play a major role in the positioning of individuals. In this chapter I explore the concept of intersectionality and use it to examine how race, gender and class impact on the experiences of non-white groups working in universities in the UK and the US.

What is intersectionality?

Intersectionality is an approach which explores how overlapping or intersecting identities affect the experiences of individuals in society. Discourses of inequality cannot simply be explained by one single factor (such as race), other competing factors operate to produce different outcomes of social and power relations. Intersectionality enables us to explore how experiences are affected by different competing identities and how these impact to exclude individuals in society.

The concept of intersectionality was first introduced by the scholar Kimberlé Crenshaw. Crenshaw[1] critically addressed the essentialist model and argued that one single identity or axis such as race or gender alone is not enough to explain and interrogate individual experiences. Crenshaw suggested that rather than having a one-dimensional approach, multiple dimensions which intersect and interweave provide a better understanding of the experiences of individuals, particularly in relation to exploring inequalities in society. Crenshaw argues that her 'focus on the intersections of race and gender only highlights the need to account for multiple grounds of identity when considering how the social world is constructed'.[2] Through a legal framework, Crenshaw stressed the need to explore how intersectionality affected unequal experiences in society, particularly those of black women. In order for black women to be part of a process that does not subordinate them, there is a need to understand and analyse how an intersectional approach to oppression can be used to provide a critical form of analysis emerging from racial inequality. Crenshaw further suggests that this is important because '[t]he failure of feminism to interrogate race means that the resistance strategies of feminism will often replicate and reinforce the subordination of people of color, and the failure of antiracism to interrogate patriarchy means that antiracism will frequently reproduce the subordination of women'.[3] As a result, it is necessary to understand how different competing identities impact on the lives of marginalised women: '[a] focus on the most privileged group members marginalises those who are multiply-burdened and obscures claims that cannot be understood as resulting from discrete sources of discrimination'. Crenshaw suggests that this approach enables us to have an understanding of the multiple oppressions which contribute to the complexity of identities.[4]

I suggest that the concept of intersectionality is a useful model to understand how white privilege and whiteness operate in different societal structures. I argue that whiteness takes centre stage where white identities predominate. Class and gender operate to reinforce whiteness for those in positions of power. Intersectionality is a useful concept to explore how discourses of difference interweave and intersect in modern-day 'risk society', marked by fear, turbulence and insecurity.[5] Intersectionality can be used as a model to analyse and engage with forms of difference, in which identities constantly change and evolve, at different times and in different spaces. Identities can be understood to reflect the context of specific situations based on the position of individual actors.

In the US, the concept of intersectionality stemmed from the notion that while all women share the same identity (of being black) they also have competing identities (such as their class), which differentiates their experiences. Consequently, the development of black feminism arose from the interrogation of the absence of the experiences of black women. Feminism only addressed the experiences of white, middle-class women and failed to see the impact of race and class on women's lives. Black feminism challenged mainstream feminism by arguing that the experiences women spoke of did not relate to their lives. These conflicts of feminism included a recognition that the struggle for equity was *both* racialised and gendered.[6] In addition to race and gender, intersectional approaches have included age, sexuality, language and religion. An intersectional approach enables an inclusion and interrogation of how the different identities of women affect and impact on their position in society.

In the US, it was Critical Race Theory (CRT) that used intersectionality as central to its analysis. The main focus of CRT is acknowledging and recognising that the experiences of individuals from oppressed backgrounds have been '... distorted, ignored, silenced, destroyed, appropriated, commodified and marginalised'.[7] Advocates of CRT recognise that race and racism are central to their analyses but also acknowledge that there is a need to interrogate how race and racism interweave and intersect with other identities. Bell suggests that '[w]e emphasize our marginality and try to turn it toward advantageous perspective building and concrete advocacy on behalf of those oppressed by race and other interlocking factors of gender, economic class, and sexual orientation'.[8]

Intersectionality emerged from a different movement in the UK. Discussions of difference of the feminist struggle in the UK centred around identities of difference based on how women defined themselves as 'black'.[9] Much of the black feminist movement was based on challenging essentialist perspectives based on racism and racist practices, particularly in relation to the labour market and the family unit (for example domestic violence). Intersectionality has been analysed through various different theoretical frameworks and different theorists have used it to engage and analyse issues of equity and social justice. Some have used it in relation to 'border theory' to explore how intersectionality works through different times and spaces in relation to the crossing of specific boundaries.[10] Others, such as Brah,[11] have used it in relation to the concept of 'diaspora space', particularly in relation to exploring how individuals move from one space to another through specific historical moments. Brah suggests that 'Diaspora space is the intersectionality of diaspora, border and dis/location as a point of confluence of economic, political, cultural and psychic processes'.[12] Others[13] have used 'mash up' conceptions of race and intersectionality to examine how white patriarchal structures exist in educational systems. Preston and Bhopal suggest that '… the study of race and intersectionality is one where the production of new theory, to meet the complex worlds of the empirical is called for … as new theories are created, "mashing up" traditional conceptions of "race" and intersectionality'.[14]

Intersectionality and policy making in the UK

In the UK, policy making on inclusion and equity in higher education appears to paint a positive picture. The Equality Challenge Unit (ECU) has been instrumental in advancing equality in further and higher education. The ECU works to provide advice, support and resources for universities and colleges to build an inclusive culture that values diversity and equality. 'We support universities and colleges to build an inclusive culture that values the benefits of diversity, to remove barriers to progression and success for all staff and students, and to challenge and change unfair practices that disadvantage individuals or groups'.[15]

The ECU introduced the Athena SWAN charter in 2005, which focussed on increasing the numbers of women in STEMM (science, technology, engineering, maths and medicine) subjects as well as advancing their positions in senior decision-making roles. Recently, in May 2015, the Athena SWAN charter included other non-science-based subjects such as arts, humanities, social sciences, business and law. It also expanded to include professional and support roles for staff and students of transgender identity. Consequently, the charter recognises that gender equality must be addressed more broadly and focus on progression as well as barriers that affect women's careers. The ECU point out that '[t]he Athena SWAN charter is based on ten key principles. By being part of Athena SWAN, institutions are committing to a progressive charter adopting these principles within their policies, practices, action plans and culture'.[16] The key principles of the Athena SWAN charter are: acknowledging that academia must fulfil its potential and to do so must include all individuals; addressing the career pipeline and lack of women in senior roles; addressing inequality in different academic disciplines and professional/support roles; tackling the gender pay gap; supporting women at major career trajectories; addressing short-term contracts; tackling the discrimination faced by those who identify as transgender; exploring how organisations and in particular leaders can advance change in organisations; making mainstream structural changes and exploring the intersections of different identities in relation to gender.[17] These core principles form the basis of the Athena SWAN charter. Any university can apply for the Athena SWAN charter but they must demonstrate clear evidence of how their organisation has been addressing gender inequalities and the changes they are making for the inclusion of women. Based on their applications, universities are awarded a gold, silver or bronze award. More recently, the Athena SWAN charter has been linked to securing grant funding. Consequently some funding bodies have suggested that in order for universities to receive funding they must demonstrate a commitment to addressing gender inequality by investing in the Athena SWAN charter. Research Councils UK (RCUK), the partnership of the seven leading funding councils in the UK, state that they

> expect that equality and diversity is embedded at all
> levels and in all aspects of research practice; individuals
> and organisations in receipt of research council

funding are expected to promote and lead culture change in relation to equality and diversity; training, support and evidencing good practice. RCUK will aim to be consistent in our strategy and expectations as a funder, employer and strategic partner, using common schemes and benchmarks such as Athena SWAN and HESA data.[18]

While the Athena SWAN charter has clearly been a positive move in the right direction to tackle gender inequalities, by its very nature and its application to STEMM subjects it has addressed the needs of white middle-class women. Furthermore it is only in its recent changes (since May 2015) that the award has addressed intersectional identities. The introduction of the Athena SWAN charter was an example of the privileging of whiteness and white identity since the main beneficiaries of the charter mark would be (and are) white middle-class women. This is further evidenced by recent research which demonstrates that black minority ethnic women from disadvantaged backgrounds are more likely to be under-represented in studying STEMM subjects and consequently in STEMM professions.[19]

While there have been significant advances in tackling gender inequalities in higher education, there are few initiatives which have addressed the underrepresentation of black and minority ethnic groups in universities. The Race Equality Charter, piloted in 2015 and introduced in 2016, is a significant step forward in addressing racial inequalities in higher education. In 2016 a total of 21 institutions applied for the Race Equality Charter and only eight were awarded. The Race Equality Charter mark is awarded on similar principles to the Athena SWAN charter, but its main focus is on advancing race equality. Institutions have currently only been awarded a bronze award based on demonstrating how they address racial inequalities in their institutions. The ECU states that the Race Equality Charter '... aims to improve the representation, progression and success of minority ethnic staff and students within higher education'.[20] It is underpinned by five key principles. The first principle is a recognition that racial inequalities exist in higher education and they do not take place as isolated incidents: 'Racism is an everyday facet of UK society and racial inequalities manifest themselves in everyday situations, processes and behaviours'.[21] This is a very important principle that the ECU has outlined and one that is crucial for the inclusion of black and minority ethnic groups in higher education. There is little recognition in higher education that racism exists, rather there is a sense of the liberal positioning of higher education institutions which assume racism is non-existent. The Race Equality Charter directly challenges the notion that higher education institutions are *not* racist. While much academic research evidences the persistence of covert racist behaviour, much of this is often dismissed as anecdotal or 'personal'. However, a recognition by the ECU that racism is a feature of higher education challenges the assumption that higher education institutions are 'safe spaces' in which racism does not exist.

Additional principles outlined by the ECU for the Race Equality Charter include acknowledging that higher education cannot reach its full potential unless it recognises the talents of all individuals; instigating long-term institutional change which avoids a deficit model; recognising that minority ethnic staff and students are not a homogeneous group; and analysing key data and making recommendations for good practice. These core principles are used by institutions to consider how they address institutional change.[22] The introduction of the Race Equality Charter is a significant step in addressing racial inequalities in higher education but also in challenging whiteness and white privilege in the white space of the academy.

One way in which prejudicial attitudes can be addressed in universities is through unconscious bias training. Unconscious bias is based on our background and experiences affecting the decisions and snap judgements we make about people. This often happens on an unconscious level without our realising we are making these judgements but it can also happen on a conscious level. The ECU states that there are two types of bias which may affect decision-making (such as on recruitment and promotion panels). These are unconscious and implicit bias. 'Unconscious bias refers to a bias that we are unaware of, and which happens outside of our control. It is a bias that happens automatically and is triggered by our brain making quick judgements and assessments of people and situations, influenced by our background, cultural environment and personal experiences'.[23] However, implicit bias '... questions the level to which these biases are unconscious especially as we are being made increasingly aware of them. Once we know that biases are not always implicit, we are responsible for them. We all need to recognise and acknowledge our biases and find ways to mitigate their impact on our behaviour and decisions'.[24]

Universities have a commitment to equality of opportunity. However, the mere existence of equality and diversity policies does not suggest that good practice is taking place and many universities may simply conform to a tick box exercise which gives the illusion that they are tackling racial inequality. Simply asserting a commitment to equality is different from demonstrating how equality and inclusion are practised. If universities are serious about inclusion and equality, unconscious bias training should become a mandatory exercise. In the first instance mandatory unconscious bias training should be a key requirement for those involved in recruitment and promotion panels. The need for such training can reduce bias in the shortlisting process.[25] However, mandatory unconscious bias training may create feelings of negativity towards black and minority ethnic groups.[26]

The ECU suggests that '[i]nstitutions could consider introducing training in a supportive, unthreatening environment to give staff the chance to think about their biases in a constructive way. This is especially important for people who may be undertaking important decisions such as in recruitment or admissions.[27]

Examples of good practice demonstrate that unconscious bias training can have positive effects on employee relations. Kings College (University of London), which holds a bronze Race Equality Charter mark, offers staff a programme of workshops that address unconscious bias, which include an unconscious bias tool kit, implicit association tests, an unconscious bias training pack developed by the ECU and documents which specifically address the impact of unconscious bias on recruitment and promotion processes. During 2015–16 Kings College made unconscious bias training mandatory for staff on senior grades.

'To limit the impact of unconscious bias on key decisions, the university has made attendance at unconscious bias training during the 2015/16 academic session, mandatory for all academics (senior lecturer and above) and all Professional Services Staff (grade 7 and above)'.[28]

However, there is evidence to suggest that there is little understanding on the part of senior managers about how diversity works in practice and there is often a mismatch between the views of individual staff and senior managers.[29] The perpetuation of white senior managers to reinforce the status quo and protect their own position is an example of the protection of white privilege and a reinforcement of their position of power.

The Equality Act

The Equality Act was introduced in October 2010. The Act brought together all previous forms of legislation such as the Equal Pay Act, the Sex Discrimination Act and the Race Relations Act in one single Act. The Equality Act provides a legal framework which works to protect the rights of individuals in advancing equality of opportunity. All organisations are legally bound to comply with the Equality Act. Employers and employees working in the public sector, and in private or voluntary organisations carrying out work on behalf of a public sector employer, have a legal public sector equality duty in the workplace to prevent and eliminate discrimination. Organisations must work to establish and promote equal opportunities in the workplace as well as foster positive relations between individuals from different backgrounds. The most important development of the Equality Act is the inclusion of 'protected characteristics'. Protected characteristics include race, age, disability, gender reassignment and religion/belief.

Changes made since the Equality Act was introduced include Equality Act provisions which came into force in April 2011. These include positive action on recruitment and promotion and the public sector equality duty. 'Public bodies have to consider all individuals when carrying out their day to day work – in shaping policy, in delivering services and in relation to their own employees'.[30] The duty also requires public bodies to have due regard for, and to be working towards, eliminating discrimination, advancing equality of opportunity and fostering positive relationships between individuals when they carry out their duties. While there have been significant advances in policy making for the inclusion of black and minority ethnic academics in higher education, inequalities continue to persist.

Higher education statistics in the UK (staff)

Black and minority ethnic (BME) people make up 14% of the total minority ethnic population in England and Wales.[31] The proportion of staff in higher education who were UK BME increased from 4.8% in 2003/04 to 6.7% in 2013/14 (representing a 39.6% increase from 2003/04 levels). In the same period, the proportion of staff who were non-UK BME increased from 3.8% to 5.0%.

BME academic staff are less likely to be in senior managerial roles. For example, among UK academic staff only 3.9% of BME staff were in senior managerial positions. Around one in five Chinese (22.7%), other (21.5%), Asian (20.7%) and white (19.7%) UK academics were in the top academic pay spine range of £57,032 and above. In contrast, only 8.9% of black and 15.2% of mixed UK academic staff were in this pay spine range. Furthermore, a total of 13,270 professors are white compared with a total of 1,050 who are from a BME background, of which only 70 are black.[32]

While there is evidence to suggest that policy making regarding inclusion and diversity has been positive, this has focussed on gender equality at the expense of intersectional identities. Black and minority ethnic women are the most disadvantaged groups in higher education; they are less likely to be professors and face greater barriers to promotion compared with their white colleagues. They are more likely to be ruled out for promotion and feel they have to be 'twice as good' as their white colleagues.[33] There is also evidence to suggest that black and minority ethnic academics, particularly women, are made to feel they do not belong in the white space of the academy.[34]

The academy works to protect its own image – one of white privilege. It works to maintain this image by excluding –

(overtly and covertly) – black and minority ethnic groups from occupying positions of power in the hierarchy of the white academy. On the one hand universities promote an inclusive agenda which emphasises equity and diversity, yet on the other hand there is little academic attention given to such debates. In many departments those who work on these issues report their work being marginalised and sidelined. As a result of this marginalisation there is evidence to suggest that black and minority ethnic academics would consider a move to overseas higher education, particularly the US, where they would feel valued.[35]

Whiteness operates in the form of white academics having access to a 'network of knowns' with whom they can identify, communicate and establish access to particular strategies that are needed to progress in the academy. Access to white privilege enables this process to take place for white academics, who are able to access the correct set of unspoken criteria which enable them to secure promotions and positions of power in the academy. Clearly, the evidence suggests that universities fail to represent the communities they serve. There is a need for universities to outline how they address inequalities and a specific recognition of the valuing of diversity for all members of staff.

In the following section I explore two case studies which examine the impact of intersectional identities and how they affect the experiences of black and minority ethnic academics in the UK and the US.

BERNADETTE: BLACK, FEMALE AND WORKING CLASS

Bernadette describes herself as a black Caribbean working-class female. She has been an academic all of her working life and enjoys her job. She works in a large post-1992 university[36] on the outskirts of a large city. She likes teaching and especially enjoys engaging with her students. She describes herself as being ambitious but not someone who 'always needs to have the limelight, I want to be successful but not in a way that draws too much attention to me'. This attitude was based on her experience of being the only black Caribbean member of staff in her department. She felt that while she had been promoted to professor she still struggled with her positioning in the academy. She referred to this as one of being an outsider who was often on the margins of the department.

> 'Sometimes I think about how I fit into my department and how I fit into my university. There are times when I feel very fortunate to have the job that I have when I teach my students and then they graduate, that's a real achievement because I think that I have had a hand in that. Other times, I don't feel like I do fit in. When I am part of the graduation ceremony it is only me and I have to count how many black people there are, that makes me feel as though perhaps this is not a place for us [black people].'

Bernadette spoke about how she was the first person in her family to attend university. She felt that the university was as an elite institution that was attended by those from privileged, middle-class backgrounds. She did not feel that going to university was something that someone of her background – being black and working class – could ever do.

> 'I remember my parents thinking and saying to me that I was very fortunate I was able to get to university, but they also saw it as this unknown quantity, because they didn't know what to expect and what it entailed. I also saw it the same way because none of my parents or my family had been to university themselves. We kind of saw it as something that mainly white middle class families did, not something that ordinary people like us from working class backgrounds did.'

Bernadette felt that her race, gender and class dictated how she was positioned in the academy and that her difference disadvantaged her and was used to position her as an outsider.

> 'I know that universities are mainly white, they are populated on the whole by white, male and pale faces. This is something that I have noticed, all of the senior teams are white men and most of them are middle class. It's the way that universities work, they have certain types of people who are at the top and then this filters down and has a domino effect. So they end up recruiting other white people who look like them and think like them. But this is not always represented in the student body. Here, we have

a diverse student body and that's when I see my identity as being an advantage. Some of the black and Asian students see me and think that they can also be successful if they want to become an academic.'

Bernadette explained how she experienced processes of exclusion and marginalisation in the white space of the university and how these manifested in covert, nuanced ways.

'It is very interesting and I know that other people have said this, but I can really relate to these experiences. So for example, you go to a meeting where people don't know you and they silently treat you in a certain way. It's kind of hidden the way the behaviour happens – and I don't even know if people know they are doing it. They kind of ignore you and make you feel as though you have nothing to contribute, they don't make eye contact with you – which is a way of saying I don't care what your opinions are. It's a way of saying, we don't want you here, this is not a space that we allow you to be in. It is our space and you are trespassing.'

Bernadette's description demonstrates how she is treated as an outsider because of her identity as a black working-class woman and because of the predominance of white privilege in the white space of the university. Such instances of subtle, covert behaviours have been well documented, particularly in relation to the use of micro aggressions. Sue et al suggest that '[r]acial micro aggressions are brief and commonplace daily verbal, behavioural, or environmental indignities, whether intentional or unintentional that communicate hostile, derogatory or negative racial slights and insults toward people of colour. Perpetrators of micro aggressions are often unaware that they engage in such communications when they interact with racial/ethnic minorities'.[37] Bernadette's explanations demonstrate how the use of micro aggressions by her white colleagues worked to perpetuate whiteness and white privilege, even though at times she felt her colleagues were unaware of their actions.

'There are some times when I think people don't know what they are doing, but isn't that just letting them off the hook? There are other times when it is very obvious and clear to me that they know what they are doing and they do those things because they want to show you that they have more power than you. They make you feel as though you don't belong in that space because it should be *their* space, theirs to occupy and own and not yours.'

Bernadette also felt that she was on the margins of her department when others discussed having access to networks which enabled them to develop external relationships with academics outside of their own institution. Bernadette was excluded from such discussions and felt this was entirely to do with her race and her working-class identity.

'I see it all around me, I see my white colleagues being given advice on who to approach, which funding body to apply to and which journals to publish in. They are able to identify with each other because they are from similar backgrounds – they do not just share a white identity, they also share a class identity where there are certain types of ways of doing things. All of these shared things mean they do not feel threatened and they feel accepted. I don't fit into that neat category of being like them, so I am always on the outside of that. And because of that, I am excluded.'

Being a black working-class woman, Bernadette did not share ways of being, doing and knowing that her white, middle-class colleagues shared. Consequently, her access to vital knowledge which would contribute to a successful career trajectory in the academy was missing and placed her at a disadvantage. The shared identity of whiteness enabled her colleagues to support each other and the identity of whiteness worked to perpetuate and reinforce white privilege to maintain the academy as a white space.

JULIAN: BLACK, MALE AND GAY

Julian describes himself as a black African American working-class gay male. He identifies himself as 'non-privileged'. He works in a non-research-intensive university in the mid-west in the US. Both his parents are from manual working-class backgrounds and neither of his parents went to university. His older brother also attended university and is a teacher. His sister is a nurse. Julian did not feel as though he belonged in the academy.

'As a black African American working class male I feel I occupy a marginalised place. I know that there are stereotypes of black African American men being seen as a threat and there are examples of how that is translated such as through the media. That tends to be the way we are portrayed. Being a gay man, I think I sit outside of that, but to others I still occupy that space because I am a black male. Being a black man who is gay is way out of people's mindset, they don't associate black masculinity and being gay together – or in the same way.'

While Julian felt his sexuality defined him and distinguished him from others, it was the fact that he was black that separated him from his colleagues.

'I know that my sexuality is seen as a threat to some but it's because I am black first that is seen as the threat. I am also from a working class background and so not seen as the way that some of my colleagues who are black and middle class are seen. But it is because I am a black African American man that is the threat. My visible identity of being black is one that you can see and one that is there for all to see so that is how I am judged. You cannot see that I am gay, and that can be something I can hide but I cannot hide my black identity – it is what you see first and foremost about me and it is from that identity that you will judge me.'

Julian suggested that the presence of a black academic elite in the US was influenced by class positioning. While the social-class background of respondents was crucial to how they were positioned in the academy, a higher social class did not preclude or dominate the identity of whiteness.

'I know that in all universities in the US – unless they are HBCUs (Historically Black Colleges and Universities) whiteness predominates. It works in such a way that is silent but loud at the same time. So you know it's there lingering in the background but then comes to bite you in the face if it needs to. We kinda know that we are not in a prominent position because we are black, and it's as though that silent whiteness keeps you in your place and makes sure that *you know your place*. That's what it's meant to do – history tells us that doesn't it? The black slave and the white owner. The black slaves always knew their place.'

Julian's experience of the predominance of whiteness was described as an 'unspoken privilege' to ensure that everyone was aware of their own place in the academic hierarchy. It was a whiteness that was related to a sense of direct entitlement to a *space* (the white academy) based on a specific *privilege* (of being white).

'Universities give the impression that they take diversity issues seriously, and some make an effort to address diversity issues in different ways. They also know they have to be seen to be doing this. But if you look closely at the make-up of faculties, there is not much real evidence that issues are being addressed. That's when you know that if you were white, it would be different for you. We have seen progression here, but the colour of your skin is still the dividing factor and being white still matters more than anything else. We are a country that has always had racial tensions – and that exists everywhere.'

Julian also suggested that many of his white colleagues felt that because the US had elected a black president, racism was something of the past that no longer existed.

'There is a feeling and this feeling exists very much in the academy that because the US people have elected a black president, then we are inclusive society but this is not the case. There is the realisation that we have greater inequalities now than ever before. If you are a young black poor male you are probably more likely to be shot than you are to go to university. If anything, Obama has introduced a new way of thinking about things in which race is always there – but that is turned into a negative and not a positive. Then there is also the idea that racism is not around anymore because we have a black president. But we know that is not the case, racism is probably worse now, here in the US race will always be a problem.'

Julian did not feel that there had been much progress regarding race relations in the US and certainly did not feel that the election of a black president had created a post-racial society.

'In some ways we have gone backwards with all the killings of black men here in the US, it feels as though we are still fighting for our rights. To be black is more of a disadvantage than it has been before and those feelings translate into education when there is still the feeling that being white makes you superior. And if those feelings can happen in universities, then how do they translate on the streets where young black men are living their lives.'

Julian's feelings of the predominance of whiteness created a sense of alienation for him and also for many of the black young men he was referring to. Racism remains endemic in US society and whiteness continues to operate to exclude black groups from the best jobs, access to healthcare and the best education.

Conclusions

The chapter has argued that class and gender play a key role in the positioning of black and minority ethnic men and women and stereotypes operate to marginalise minority ethnic groups. Higher education is an example of how whiteness and white privilege continue to dominate. The academy works to perpetuate white privilege and protect the position of white groups who hold the most senior roles. Consequently, the identity of being white dominates how universities portray their image to the outside world. Universities play the diversity card, yet this is not reflected in practice. Those in senior academic positions – namely white groups – work to maintain the status quo and protect their own positions of power and privilege. Unequal processes and structures maintain and perpetuate white privilege with the illusion that diversity and equity are being addressed.

FIVE

Race, schooling and exclusion

This chapter will examine how black and minority ethnic groups are disadvantaged in their schooling experiences. It explores how from an early age unequal participation and access to education shapes the lives of young people and affects the decisions they make in relation to higher education and transitions into the labour market. The chapter argues that children's experiences of schooling are affected by their race and, in turn, their class. The chapter draws on case study examples of the experiences of black and minority ethnic teachers to explore how the exclusionary processes of schools work to disadvantage black and minority ethnic groups. The chapter focusses primarily on the UK experience with a brief view of the US position.

Education for all?

1985 saw the publication of the Swann Report,[1] which argued for 'Education for all' yet we continue to live in a society in which inequalities in school experiences predominate. School experiences are crucial in the transition to further and higher education and access to the labour market, yet black and minority ethnic groups continue to remain disadvantaged in these transitions. Alexander et al state:

> Education remains a primary area for both the maintenance of entrenched racial stereotyping and discrimination, on the one hand, and anti-racist activism on the other. Concerns over structural racism, low educational attainment, poor teacher

expectations and stereotyping, ethnocentric curricula and high levels of school exclusions for some groups remain entrenched features of our school system.[2]

Inclusive policy making?

The Race Relations Amendment Act,[3] which was introduced after the Sir William Macpherson Report,[4] made public bodies accountable for race equality. Public bodies (including schools) had a duty to promote race equality and implement the policies and programmes that demonstrated this. Schools were expected to record and monitor racist incidents and send these to their local educational authority in order that ethnic monitoring of such incidents could take place. However, subsequent governments have removed this duty and replaced it within the Equality Act.[5] The Equality Act introduced a public sector equality duty (PSED), which came into effect in 2011. The PSED '... applies to public bodies, including maintained schools and academies, and extends to certain protected characteristics – race, disability, sex, age, religion or belief, sexual orientation, pregnancy and maternity and gender reassignment'.[6] Public bodies such as schools are required to: eliminate discrimination and other conduct that is prohibited by the Act; advance equality of opportunity; and foster good relations between people who share a protected characteristic and those who do not. Schools are expected to have 'due regard' for these elements in the following ways:

1. 'Due regard' must be taken into consideration when decisions are made, and an assessment must be made as to the impact this may or may not have on those with protected characteristics.
2. Schools should consider equality implications when they make policy decisions and these must be reviewed on a regular basis.
3. The PSED must be integrated into the carrying out of the school's functions; it cannot be just a tick box exercise or follow a particular process.
4. Schools cannot delegate responsibility for this duty to anyone else.[7]

However, schools are not required to keep records of how they have been actively addressing their equality duties, though the Department for Education (DfE) does recommend it is 'good practice' to do so. Schools are expected to publish information to demonstrate how they are complying with the PSED and to prepare and publish equality objectives. Previously, schools were required to publish equality schemes in relation to race, gender and disability. However the PSED no longer requires schools to do this. Consequently, the attention given to racial inequalities as a single significant determiner of social inequality has been eroded. As a result, schools have no legal obligation to ensure that equality based on race is addressed and consequently, a race equality agenda has been pushed into insignificance.

Educational achievement by ethnicity

Recent figures[8] suggest that the numbers of black and minority ethnic pupils attending schools in England and Wales have increased since January 2014. In state-funded primary schools, 30.4% of pupils were from black and minority ethnic backgrounds and 26.6% in secondary schools. These proportions have increased from 29.5% and 25.3% respectively since January 2014. The ethnic groups with the largest increases from January 2014 to January 2015 were white British, any other white background, Asian and Chinese. In secondary schools, the ethnic groups with the largest numbers between 2014 and 2015 were white British, Asian, any other background and mixed.[9]

In terms of GCSE performance, Figure 5.1 demonstrates that Chinese students are the highest performing ethnic group. A total of 74.4% of Chinese pupils achieved at least five A★ C GCSEs (or equivalent) grades including English and maths. This is 17.8 percentage points above the national average (56.6%).[10] A total of 72.9% of pupils from an Indian background achieved at least 5 A★ C GCSEs (or equivalent) grades including English and maths. This is 16.3 percentage points above the national average. In comparison, a total of 47% of black Caribbean pupils achieved at least 5 A★–C GCSEs (or equivalent) grades including English and maths, 9.6 percentage points below the national average. Furthermore, only 8.2% of Gypsy/Roma pupils achieved at least 5 A*–C GCSEs or equivalent grades including English and maths, a considerable 48.4 percentage points below the national average.[11]

Figure 5.1: Percentage of pupils achieving 5+ A*–C GCSEs (or equivalent) grades including English and mathematics, England, 2013–14

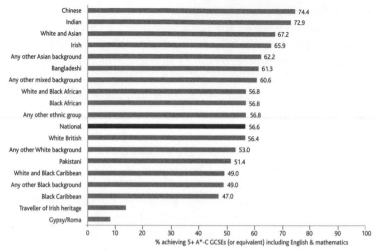

Source: DfE, 2015a, *GCSE and equivalent attainment by pupil characteristics, 2013 to 2014* (Revised), SFR06/2015, London: DfE.

A changing school system?

Recent changes in the school system, with the introduction of free schools, academies and faith schools, have introduced greater complexity in how equality issues are addressed. There is evidence to suggest that the introduction of different schools does not increase real school choice for parents from black and minority ethnic backgrounds.[12] For example, individuals from black and minority ethnic communities are less likely to engage with the free schools programme and little effort has been made by those involved in the introduction of free schools to encourage black and minority ethnic parents to get involved.[13] Recent research has found that many free schools were not adhering to the legal requirements of equality and diversity as outlined in the Equality Act[14] and they were less likely to publish their equality objectives compared with academies and maintained schools. The research also found that most free schools were unaware of the Equality Act and the PSED and were not demonstrating a clear commitment to racist bullying and harassment.[15]

The introduction of different types of schools has encouraged a process of deregulation and lack of monitoring, particularly in relation to how they function and their implementation of policies which address equality and diversity. Such an approach encourages schools to take individual measures to cater for their school community, rather than fostering a collective responsibility which tackles inequalities in society. The movement from regulation to a gradual process of deregulation suggests that schools are not obliged to address issues of equality and diversity.

Inequality and disadvantage: school exclusions

There is recent evidence to suggest an overall decrease in the total number and rate of permanent school exclusions in England since 2015, however the numbers of fixed-term exclusions in primary schools have seen an increase.[16] A recent Equalities and Human Rights Commission (EHRC) report found that pupils from ethnic minority backgrounds experience disproportionate rates of exclusion compared with those from other ethnic groups, with white pupils from disadvantaged backgrounds also having high rates. The EHRC state that '[i]n England, Black Caribbean, mixed white/Black Caribbean, Gypsy/Roma and Traveller children continue to experience disproportionate rates of exclusions'.[17] Within this group, Gypsy/Roma Traveller children have the highest rates of both permanent and fixed-term exclusions and black Caribbean and mixed white/black Caribbean children have rates of permanent exclusion about three times that of the pupil population as a whole – which is shocking! Pupils of Asian and Chinese backgrounds, however, have the lowest rates of exclusion.

Bullying

There is evidence to suggest that children are more likely to be bullied because of their race, religion or ethnicity[18] and there is a plethora of research evidence to show that being bullied has significant impacts on children's school experiences, particularly in relation to educational achievement, confidence and self-esteem. It can also impact negatively on future life experiences.[19] Children who experience bullying are less likely to be engaged in positive friendship networks, which can have a negative impact on their educational achievements[20] and lead to mental health problems in later life.[21] As discussed above, schools are no longer required to record incidents of racist bullying. Consequently, racist incidents are under-reported and under-recorded; this may be due to lack of leadership in schools and lack of staff training in how to deal with such issues.[22] A recent report by the Office for Standards in Education (OFSTED) indicated that racist language in schools is commonplace.[23] There has also been evidence to suggest an increase in requests for counselling for racist and religiously motivated bullying from school children. Over the period 2012/13 a total of 1,400 young people across Britain contacted ChildLine to report racist bullying. This is a shocking 69% increase within a year.[24] There have been similar findings in Wales[25] and Scotland.[26]

British values?

In 2014 the Department of Education introduced statutory guidance to promote and teach fundamental British values as part of the school curriculum. 'All maintained schools must meet the requirements set out in Section 78 of the Education Act 2001 and promote the spiritual, moral, social and cultural (SMSC) development of their pupils. Through ensuring pupils' SMSC development, schools can also demonstrate they are actively promoting fundamental British values'.[27]

But what are *British* values? How are they defined? What exactly is *British* culture and how can this be taught in schools? Are these based on interpretations of British imperialism and/ or colonialism? Or are they something else? The DfE states:

Schools should promote the fundamental British values of democracy, the rule of law, individual liberty and mutual respect and tolerance of those with different faiths and beliefs … actively promoting the values means challenging the opinions or behaviours in schools that are contrary to fundamental British values. Attempts to promote systems that undermine fundamental British values would be completely at odds with schools' duty to provide SMSC.[28]

As part of their OFSTED inspections schools are assessed on how they are teaching 'British values'. 'OFSTED inspectors must consider pupils' spiritual, moral, social and cultural (SMSC) development when forming a judgement of a school'.[29]

The SMSC policy was introduced in the wake of the 'Trojan Horse' affair in Birmingham, UK following allegations that Muslims were taking over schools in Birmingham with a view to teaching children fundamental radical Muslim values. After an investigation into the schools, the Education Select Committee found that apart from one incident in one school, 'no evidence of extremism or radicalisation was found by any of the inquiries in any of the schools involved'.[30] What was found, however, was a lack of coordination between the different agencies involved in the investigation (the DfE, OFSTED, the Education Funding Agency and Birmingham City Council). As a result, the DfE concluded: 'As today's report recognises, we are tackling this problem at both ends: taking determined action where we find areas of concern, and building resilience in the system by putting the active promotion of fundamental British values at the heart of our plan for education'.[31]

Then Prime Minister David Cameron published an article for the *Mail Online* in 2014 prior to the introduction of the SMSC policy in which he said:

In recent years, we have been in danger of sending out a worrying message: that if you don't want to believe in democracy, that's fine; that if equality isn't your bag, don't worry about it; that if you're completely intolerant of others, we will still tolerate you. As I've said before, this has not just led to division, it has allowed extremism – of both the violent and non-violent kind – to flourish. So I believe we need to be far more muscular in promoting British values and the institutions that uphold them. That's what a genuinely liberal country does: it believes in certain values and actively promotes them. It says to its citizen; this is what defines us as a society.[32]

However, many teachers whose responsibility it is to teach 'British values' feel uncomfortable doing so. At the recent National Union of Teachers (NUT) conference in March 2016, teachers said that teaching 'British values' was an act of 'cultural supremacism' in which the teaching of 'fundamental British values sets an inherent cultural supremacism particularly in the context of multicultural schools and the wider picture of migration'.[33] Consequently, the NUT passed a motion to replace the concept of 'British values' with one which focusses on 'international rights' policies that welcome migrants and refugees into Britain where members were encouraged to 'gather and collate materials on migrants and refugees' to be used in schools.

At the NUT conference, Christopher Denson, a teacher from Coventry, said that teaching fundamental values to students in schools was difficult as many of the students he teaches had ancestors who had experienced British colonialism. He said:

The inherent cultural supremacism in that term is both unnecessary and unacceptable. And seen with the Prevent agenda, it belies the most thinly veiled racism and a conscious effort to divide communities ... it's our duty to push a real anti-racist work in all schools. And that doesn't mean talk of tolerating other's views, but genuine, inclusive anti-racist work.[34]

However, Chris McGovern from the Campaign for Real Education said:

Teachers should not be playing the role of fifth columnists in the ideological war currently being fought over our national identity and national sovereignty. Teaching children that British values are part of cultural supremacism will at best, make them feel guilty about being British and at worst, radicalise them in order to 'make up' for the sins of their fathers.[35]

The NUT also demanded that the government withdraw the Prevent strategy, which since 2015 has obliged teachers to refer pupils to the police if they suspect them of participating in terrorist or radical behaviour (see below). Following the NUT conference, the *Mail Online* featured an article under the headline 'Militant teachers demand schools stop promoting "British values" as it makes children from other cultures feel inferior'.[36]

Citizenship

In 2013, the DfE introduced statutory guidelines for the teaching of citizenship in schools for pupils at key stages 3 and 4 (ages 11–16). All schools are expected to teach pupils about the meaning, value and implementation of citizenship in society. 'A high-quality citizenship education helps to provide pupils with knowledge, skills and understanding to prepare them to play a full and active part in society. In particular, citizenship education should foster pupils' keen awareness and understanding of democracy, government and how laws are made and upheld'.[37] The emphasis on citizenship was based on pupils being able to understand how the UK is governed and how citizens participate in the political system; to develop an understanding of the rule of law; to develop an interest in participating in society, for example through volunteering; and to enable students to think critically about politics as well as being able to plan for future financial needs. Citizenship continues to be taught in schools, not as a separate subject but one that is subsumed under PSHE (personal, social and health education). Citizenship is also used to teach about British values and used in conjunction with the Prevent strategy.[38]

Prevent

The Prevent Duty Guidance states: 'Section 26 of the Counter-Terrorism and Security Act 2015 places a duty on certain bodies ("specified authorities" listed in schedule 6 to the Act), in the exercise of their functions, to have due regard to the need to prevent people from being drawn into terrorism'. This guidance is issued under section 29 of the Act. The Act states that 'authorities subject to the provisions must have due regard to this guidance when carrying out the duty'.[39] Schools, colleges and higher education institutions are all expected to comply with the Prevent duty. For schools, this means: ... it is essential that staff are able to identify children who may be vulnerable to radicalisation and know what to do when they are identified. Protecting children from the risk of radicalisation should be seen as part of schools' and childcare providers' wider safeguarding duties, and is similar in nature to protecting children from other harms (for example drugs, gangs, neglect, sexual exploitation), whether these come from within their family or are the product of outside influences. Schools and childcare providers can also build pupils' resilience to radicalisation by promoting fundamental British values and enabling them to challenge extremist views.[40]

Clearly there are issues as to how 'extremism' and 'radicalisation' are defined and whether it is the role of teachers to identify children and young people whom they perceive to be displaying these traits. Furthermore, how can teachers be trained to identify such traits?

The teaching of fundamental 'British values' and the introduction of the Prevent duty suggests the narrative and rhetoric of race has been pushed into a new direction – one that is associated with terrorism, fear and othering. Educational policy making has shifted from addressing the underachievement of some minority ethnic groups and challenging how minority ethnic groups are being marginalised (particularly in relation to bullying and racism in schools) – to a discourse based on a 'blame culture' in which black and minority ethnic groups are seen as posing a threat to the social order of UK society. A shift in the discourse from addressing racism and racist processes towards one which prioritises marginalisation of the 'other' is one that has surfaced in a climate of insecurity, fear and risk. Crozier suggests that,

> [t]he discourse around 'difference' has been fuelled and polarised by the implication that BME (Black and minority ethnic) differences are negative, lacking value and at times dangerous. The focus on terrorism which has now encroached on schools, has heightened the moral panic and in particular exacerbates Islamophobia ... this discourse takes the 'them and us' perspective to another level.[41]

Rather than challenging such stereotypes, this blame discourse reinforces 'otherness' as being associated with terrorism. The predominance of whiteness and white privilege dictates that those who do not hold 'British values', those who are 'different' and those who do not conform to 'Britishness' pose a threat. The Prevent strategy also assumes that there is a direct link between radicalisation and terrorism, however there is evidence to suggest that this is rarely the case.[42] The moral panic surrounding terrorism and its link to Muslim identity has created a society in which the 'other' is identified as the enemy fighting against 'British values', perpetuating radical Islam and engaging in terrorist activities.

As a result of such policy making, shockingly over 900 children were identified as being 'at risk of radicalisation' from April 2012 to April 2015. This included 84 children under the age of 12 and one as young as three.[43] The Prevent agenda has further changed the teacher–pupil relationship from one based on support to one in which teachers are expected to be vigilant spies looking for signs of radicalisation and terrorism. The discourse of schools which focussed on raising the standards of black and minority ethnic groups has moved to one in which such groups are defined as the enemy.

The lack of a clear measurement of the effectiveness of the Prevent agenda and its discrimination against Muslim groups is evident in how the policy itself is used. Furthermore, critics suggest it can be counterproductive in achieving its aims. Maina

Kiai, a Kenyan lawyer who has served on the United Nations Committee on the rights to freedom of peaceful assembly (Office of the United Nations High Commissioner for Human Rights [OHCHR]) as a special rapporteur since 2011 has said that '[b]y dividing, stigmatising and alienating segments of the population, Prevent could end up promoting extremism, rather than countering it'. He suggests that Prevent will have the effect of causing fear among many families who will be afraid to discuss any issues of religion, for fear of reprisal. 'The spectre of Big Brother is so large, in fact, that I was informed that some families are afraid of discussing the negative effects of terrorism in their own homes, fearing their children will talk about it at school and have their intentions misconstrued'.[44] David Anderson QC (Independent Reviewer of Terrorist Legislation) suggests that an independent review of the Prevent strategy is urgently needed, together with a government-wide initiative that actively encourages mainstream political engagement from young British Muslims.[45]

The moral panic surrounding Muslims as terrorists is not just confined to the UK. I have discussed the rhetoric of Donald J Trump in the presidential election campaign in the US in Chapter Two. A further recent example of this is the case of Ahmed Mohamed who was suspended from school and later arrested for bringing a hoax bomb to his suburban Dallas high school in September 2015. Ahmed made a clock from a plastic pencil box, electrical wire and other electrical hardware he had obtained from his parents' garage, and took it school to show his teachers. During a media frenzy, the family had to leave the area after receiving death threats. They have subsequently filed a lawsuit against the school for violating their son's civil rights. The case continues.[46]

Teachers and a white curriculum

There is a great deal of evidence to suggest that teachers are not fully equipped to understand the experiences of black and minority ethnic pupils in the classroom. Many teachers from white backgrounds fail to recognise their own whiteness and their own white privilege and how this affects their teaching in the classroom.[47]

Teachers also have stereotypes about particular black and minority ethnic groups, with Indian and Chinese students seen as 'high achievers' and black students seen as 'disruptive and lazy',[48] which results in black students being placed in lower streams than their white counterparts.[49] Solomon et al[50] suggest that it is the role of teacher training programmes to enable trainees to examine their own 'racial and ascription and social positioning' and how this affects what takes place in the classroom and in their teaching. Stereotypical assumptions of what is expected from some children (black) compared with others (white) takes place in which some students are *expected* to fail while others are expected to succeed. Much of the research points to the lack of training offered to trainee teachers in recognising the difference between pupils and developing strategies to increase educational attainment for all, rather than the few.[51] Furthermore, teachers are not fully equipped to deal with the racism that pupils face in the classroom.[52]

Many teachers lack knowledge of the history and contribution of black and minority ethnic communities to the UK. Consequently, the contribution of these communities to the UK historical experience is vastly selective. Doharty[53] suggests that the curriculum's focus on ethnocentrism presents a skewed view of history. White British history is considered the norm and black history is seen as being on the margins. The separation of white and black history into different specific areas '... exposes "white" students to a parochial, liberal (often male) history curriculum characterised by "white" success while Black and minority ethnic students face the reinforcing messages that "their" histories belong on the periphery outside of British history'.[54] The teaching of white history is an example of white privilege in which students are taught that black history is secondary to that of whiteness and white experience. There is ample evidence to suggest that black and minority ethnic groups have made a vast contribution to the history of the UK.[55]

The predominance of whiteness, such as only teaching white history in the classroom, influences the type of knowledge that is considered legitimate. Rather than focussing on processes of structural racism, marginalisation and exclusion, schools have shifted their focus towards a perspective that uses cultural stereotypes to label and pathologise non-white groups. The process of 'othering' that takes place within this rhetoric perpetuates and reinforces the notion that whiteness is superior and black and minority ethnic identity is measured against this superiority. As Crozier[56] suggests:

> Rather than focus on a divisive ethnocentric curricula, such as the focus on 'British values', schools need to assert the importance of critically engaging with universal values and exploring knowledge that is more appropriate to an ethnically diverse and rich society of the 21st century. Developing a critical anti-racist pedagogy would be more appropriate and beneficial for all students in their preparation for citizenship in a global cosmopolitan society.

The US experience

In the US, students do not sit GCSE examinations but graduate from high school. The National Centre for Education Statistics uses two indicators to measure high school completion; the average freshman graduation rate (AFGR) and the adjusted cohort graduation rate (ACGR). Both of these measures are able to determine the percentage of public school students who have obtained a high school diploma within four years of starting ninth grade. The difference between the two measures is that the AFGR is an estimate of the four-year graduation rate derived from aggregate student enrolment data and the ACGR uses detailed student-level data to determine the percentage of students who graduate within four years of starting ninth grade.[57] The data suggests that in 2013–14 the ACGRs for American Indian/Alaska Native (70%), black (73%) and Hispanic students (76%) were below the national average of 82%. The ACGRs for white students (87%) and Asian/Pacific Islander (89%) students were above the national average.

In terms of maths and English, the National Centre for Education Statistics (NCES) data suggests that closing the

Figure 5.2: Adjusted cohort graduation rate (ACGR) for public high school students, by race/ethnicity: school year 2013–14

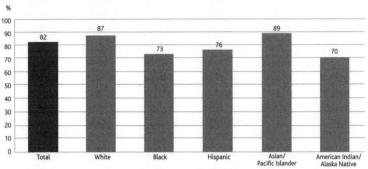

Note: The Bureau of Indian Education and Puerto Rico were not included in US four-year ACGR estimates. Race categories exclude persons of Hispanic ethnicity. Source: US Department of Education, Office of Elementary and Secondary Education, Consolidated State Performance Report, 2013–14. See *Digest of Education Statistics 2015.*

achievement gaps for different ethnic groups is a goal of national and local US policies. 'In 2015 and in previous assessment years since 1990, the average mathematics scores for white students in grades 4 and 8 have been higher than the scores of their black and Hispanic peers. For both grades, there was some narrowing of the racial/ethnic achievement gaps since the 1990s'.[58] Similarly for English, the NCES states:

> From 1992 through 2015, the average reading scores for white 4th and 8th graders were higher than those of their black and Hispanic peers. Although the white-black and White–Hispanic achievement gaps did not change measurably from 2013 to 2015 at either grade 4 or 8, some of the racial/ethnic achievement gaps have narrowed since 1992.[59]

The data suggests that black students and those from Hispanic backgrounds are not performing as well as their white counterparts. Further inequalities suggest that black students are four times more likely to be suspended than white students. The US Department of Education found that suspensions overall had decreased by nearly 20% between 2011–12 and 2013–14 but there were differences across ethnic groups. From pre-school, black children are 3.6 times more likely to receive one or more suspensions compared with white children. Black girls represent 20% of female pre-school enrolment but account for 54% of the suspensions. Black students were also twice as likely to be expelled compared with white students.[60]

Inequalities in the US continue to persist despite significant advances in race equality policy making. The race achievement gap has barely narrowed in the last 50 years between white and black students.[61] There are many reasons for the poor performance of black children in schools in the US. An increase in school segregation, harsher discipline for black children[62] and lack of investment in schools in poor black areas[63] in which highly qualified teachers do not want to work[64] are some of the reasons given for the underachievement of black groups in the US. There is evidence to suggest that teachers are not prepared to teach in diverse schools and address issues of race and racism.[65] McGee argues that 'Racial biases often place undue burdens on black students who already experience multiple forms of discrimination and prejudice, while the educational and social institutions they learn in, perpetuate white privilege'.[66]

The following section presents two case studies of black and minority ethnic teachers working in schools in England.

CASE STUDY: JEANNETTE

Jeannette describes herself as a black working-class Caribbean woman whose main passion was to be a teacher. Jeanette teaches in an inner-city, ethnically mixed primary school. She chose to teach in such a school as she wanted her experiences of teaching to be reflective of her own life, which was based on living in a diverse city consisting of a mixed population of people from around the world who spoke many different languages. She felt that her teacher training course did not adequately address issues of multiculturalism and inclusion.

'I remember when we were taught a session on inclusion and diversity and that was it. I know it's changed a lot now and they try to do more, but then it was nothing and I was a bit worried, thinking how are students going to understand some of the things that black parents talk about when they come into the school? Like they want their kids to do really well, but the stereotypes say something different.'

Jeannette did not think that teachers were prepared to understand or address some of the issues that many black and minority ethnic children faced and how racism affected their school experiences.

'A lot of the people on my teacher training course were white and they were all from very privileged backgrounds – their parents were teachers and they came from families were everyone went to university. That was not the case for me, I had to work hard to get here and I think that struggle is missed, it says something about why you decide to become a teacher. For me it was about helping those students whose parents can't read to them or can't spend time with them because they have to go to work.'

Jeannette spoke about particular stereotypes teachers had of certain children.

'All of the teachers have ways they think about the children. There are some of the black children in this school whose parents have had a hard time and they struggle to get their children in to school because they have other problems at home that they have to deal with. Some of the teachers here will immediately dismiss them and say it's part of what black people do, their culture – it's the way they are. But that's not the case, it has nothing to do with ethnicity. The parents have problems and we should try and understand those problems and support them when we can. It also stems from the particular stereotypes we have of black families. It's as if they are expected to be from single parent families, not working etc so an assumption exists that they won't do well at school.'

These stereotypes were also related to the expectations teachers had of white, middle-class children who were expected to succeed.

'I can see how it works here in the school. The white parents – those who are middle class – are able to chat to the teacher when they drop their kids off – they feel comfortable and are not threatened by the teachers. The teacher will make a judgement about that child because the child comes from a white middle class family and they know they have spoken to the parent. They will expect that child to do well. With some of the black children whose parents either don't drop them off or they come in on their own, they don't have that connection to the teacher. So the teacher will assume that the parent doesn't care.'

Parents' (particularly mothers') use of their social and cultural capital to advocate for their children's education has been seen to be influential in how teachers treat parents and their children.[67] The predominance of white privilege in relation to class privilege ensures that children are judged favourably and will achieve successful outcomes based on the expectations of their teachers. Asked if this was a form of racism, Jeanette responded:

'I'm not sure if it's a form of overt racism, but it's a form of discrimination in which teachers make certain judgements about the kids based on their ethnicity. There are still presumptions made about you based on the colour of your skin, this may not be something that we talk about anymore because we like to think that we have moved beyond that coarse way of dividing people and putting them into certain boxes. But I think it still happens, it is more disguised.'

Jeannette felt that white parents and their children were treated favourably by white teachers.

'There is a certain way that the white teachers treat the white parents – especially the professional ones who are educated. I think they might be afraid of them, so maybe treat them better or want to impress them. They also make judgements about parents based on what they think they know about the parents – and sometimes their assessments or stereotypes may not be true. I think sometimes teachers have a lot of power to make judgements and this can affect the child's whole school experience.'

Jeannette suggested that schools needed more black teachers who could act as role models for children who continued to be labelled as failures.

'We need to encourage more black students to come into the teaching profession – more men as well. The black teachers will have high expectations of the black children and this will give the children positive role models to make them want to do well at school. At the moment, there is a move away from thinking about how the ethnic background affects the child's experience, but I think we have to go back to that and think about those things, and how they can impact on the whole educational experience of a child.'

CASE STUDY: FARAH

Farah teaches in a secondary school in a small town on the outskirts of a large multicultural city in the Midlands in the UK. Farah is Muslim and wears a hijab and spoke about her experiences in relation to her religion. The school Farah teaches in is predominantly white British (85%).

'I have seen a change here in the last few years. There has been a change in what the students say and also some change in the staff. It's not what the staff say, it's what they don't say that is interesting. There is an anti-Muslim sentiment with some of the students, but I think when they are challenged about this they tend to back down. It comes from their parents who think that all Muslims are the enemy.'

Farah spoke about how changes in school policy such as the teaching of British values and the Prevent agenda had created tensions in the school.

'We now have to teach children about Britishness and we are made to think about how to identify who may be a terrorist. That is tricky because it creates certain tensions about assumptions that all Muslims are terrorists. I have heard some of the students say racist things about Muslims – especially when there has been a terrorist attack – the school does not tolerate that and we act on it, but it still happens. There are values we can teach the children inside the school, but we can't control what goes on outside. The children learn and see things outside that they bring inside the school and sometimes these can be racist.'

Farah discussed how she was treated by parents when she first arrived at the school.

'There are ways in which people treat you. Some of the year 7 parents when they first meet me, I know some of them feel uncomfortable speaking to me. To them, in a hijab I represent the enemy. Some of them are also surprised when they speak to me, I'm not sure what they expect but they are sometimes surprised by me. One good thing is that I can shatter those stereotypes they have of Muslim women being submissive and not having opinions.'

Farah's 'presentation of self' had a significant impact on how she was seen by parents and also by some students. She felt that her own identity of being a female Muslim wearing a hijab positioned her as an outsider who did not belong.

'There are those who are seen to be part of society because they are white, rich or middle class and there are others who are not part of that. It could be that you are poor or black or a different religion, but ultimately there is a feeling that you are on the outside because you are not like them. And you are always judged because of this, no matter what. It doesn't matter how liberal people are, they will always judge you based on what you look like and I will be judged for being a Muslim.'

Farah related her negative experience to current policy changes such as the Prevent agenda and the rhetoric which centred on white Britishness. Wearing clothing such as the hijab becomes a basis on which individuals – namely women – are excluded and treated as outsiders. The predominance of whiteness and white privilege articulated in policy making reinforced Farah's position as the 'other'.

Conclusions

This chapter has argued that policy making in schools, in its attempts to address issues of inclusion, has failed to achieve its aims; instead it has marginalised and alienated black and minority ethnic communities. The teaching of fundamental British values and the introduction of the Prevent strategy is an introduction of racial policies designed to alienate those who do not identify with notions of Britishness. At its core is a privileging of white ethnocentric identity, designed to marginalise and exclude black and minority ethnic groups.

Education is a space in which the norms of whiteness are reinforced and reproduced. Outsiders who do not identify with these norms ('British values') are seen as a threat. The school space is used to maintain and privilege whiteness at the same time as asserting its dominance over black and minority ethnic groups. Whiteness works to perpetuate and reinforce white racial superiority. A discussion of the failures of the education system to meet the needs of black and minority ethnic students (based on their underachievements, experiences of racism from pupils and teachers, and high rates of exclusion) threatens white privilege and white stability, and is replaced by a rhetoric that blames the 'other'.

SIX

Higher education, race and representation

This chapter will examine inequalities in higher education. Recent UK data suggests that the numbers of black and minority ethnic groups who attend university have increased, yet their access to elite Russell Group universities[1] remains low.[2] This chapter will explore why black and minority ethnic groups remain under-represented in elite Russell Group universities and suggest that processes of exclusionary practices in these universities based on white privilege exclude those from non-white backgrounds. In this chapter I suggest that processes of racial exclusion are used to maintain the elite position of universities which are based on white middle-class acceptance. As a result, such universities are able to maintain their positions of privilege. This chapter will primarily focus on the UK followed by a brief discussion of the US experience.

Ethnicity and student data

There is recent evidence to suggest that the numbers of black and minority ethnic students have shown a year on year increase, from 14.9% in 2003/4 to 20.2% a decade later.[3] Despite this increase in the overall number of black and minority ethnic undergraduate students, when their experiences are compared against standard measures of success (such as degree class attained, employment after university or progression to postgraduate study), such students do not do as well as white students.

Higher proportions of white students successfully completed their degrees in 2014-2015 (91.8%) compared with 87.9% of black and minority ethnic students.[4] In all of the UK, the number of black students who received a first-class or 2:1 degree was lower than all other ethnic groups.[5] White students (75.6%) are more likely to receive a first-class or 2:1 degree compared with black and minority ethnic students (60.4%).[6] The gap is largest in England,[7] with 76.3% of white students receiving a first or 2:1 compared with 60.3% of black and minority ethnic students.[8] The destination of leavers survey suggests that black and minority ethnic groups are more likely to be unemployed six months after graduating[9] with 61.5% of white leavers in full-time work compared with 53.9% of black and minority ethnic leavers.[10] A total of 50.0% of Asian Indian leavers were in professional full-time work, which was higher than the proportions of all other black and minority ethnic groups.[11]

The data suggests that black and minority ethnic students have a younger profile than white students: 71.8% aged 25 and under compared with 69.2% of white students.[12] Overall, within every ethnic group, black students have the highest proportion of students who are women (59.3%).[13] Students from black and minority ethnic backgrounds were more likely to be studying at MillionPlus institutions (30.4%)[14] and least likely to be studying at Russell Group universities (8.4%).[15]

While there has been a year-on-year increase in the numbers of black and minority ethnic students attending universities, there are still vast inequalities in the experiences of black and minority ethnic students compared with white students. Black and minority ethnic students are less likely than white students to attend elite Russell Group universities, less likely to leave university with a first-class or 2:1 degree and are less likely to be in employment six months after graduating.[16] There is also evidence to suggest that universities have been reluctant to think about how these aspects of inequality can be addressed to create a greater inclusive experience for those from black and minority ethnic backgrounds.[17]

Widening participation

In 1999 then Labour Prime Minister Tony Blair introduced the widening participation agenda, which outlined plans to increase the numbers of young people attending universities to 50% by 2010. The aim was to ensure that individuals from disadvantaged and less privileged backgrounds would be given equal access to university compared with those from privileged backgrounds. The emphasis on the widening participation agenda has continued with subsequent governments.[18]

The widening participation agenda, in its attempts to encourage and increase the numbers of black and minority ethnic students entering higher education, has had a significant impact in the numbers of such students attending universities. However, higher education remains highly segregated, with elite Russell Group universities continuing to be populated by white middle-class students (many of whom were privately educated). By contrast post-1992 universities continue to be populated by working-class and black and minority ethnic students.

The Independent Schools Council (ISC) represents and promotes the interests of 1,200 private schools in the UK that are members of the Council, and the wider interests of the independent school sector (that is, private, fee-paying schools outside of the state sector). In 2017 the ISC estimated that 6.5% of school children in the UK attend independent schools compared with 93% who attend state schools. Despite the very small number of children whose parents can afford to pay the substantial fees associated with a private education, a disproportionately large number of privately educated children go on to secure places at Russell Group universities, including Oxford and Cambridge. According to the 2017 ISC census 55% of privately educated children progressed to Russell Group institutions, including 6% who went to study at Oxford or Cambridge.[19]

To put this into perspective, a total of 40% of all undergraduates at Oxbridge were privately educated, suggesting that children from state schools are significantly disadvantaged on the basis of their inability to pay for a better education. Recently there have been attempts by Oxbridge to increase the numbers of students from disadvantaged backgrounds, however the evidence still suggests few children from working-class or black and minority ethnic backgrounds take up such schemes. Furthermore, teachers in state schools are less likely to encourage their brightest children to apply to Oxbridge.[20] Reay suggests that '... it seems very apparent that there are strong processes of positive discrimination at work in Oxbridge, bestowing advantage on the already advantaged'.[21] Reay goes on to argue that:

> Of the 200,000 of the nation's children who live in poor areas, 1.1 per cent get in. This is not just an issue of class; Black and Minority Ethnic (BME) students are more likely to come from a lower socio-economic background with 75 per cent of Britain's minority communities living in 88 of Britain's poorest wards.[22]

Oxbridge is an example of the perpetuation of white privilege related to wealth and class. If Oxbridge continues to be dominated by privately educated students, the elitism of such universities is perpetuated. 'Oxbridge remains the equivalent of a "finishing school" for the private school system, polishing, refining and accentuating the elitism and sense of superiority acquired in earlier schooling'.[23] A recent report published by the Social Mobility and Child Poverty commission outlines the continuing failure of Oxbridge to increase the intake of students from state schools. Noting that only one other university (Bristol) has a worse record in improving access to state students, the report noted: 'To meet their benchmarks, Oxford would need to increase the percentage of state school pupils by a quarter (24 per cent) and Cambridge by a fifth (18 per cent)'.[24]

Furthermore, the report argues that such inequalities continue, particularly in gaining access to elite, highly paid professions: '71% of senior judges, 62% of senior armed forces and 55% of civil service departmental heads attended independent schools – compared to just 7% of the population who had a private education'.[25] The report suggests that '... in every single sphere of British influence the upper echelons of power are held overwhelmingly by a small elite'.[26]

Discrimination?

Black and minority ethnic groups are less likely than their white counterparts to attend elite Russell Group universities.[27] I suggest that this demonstrates universities use mechanisms to protect and reserve places in elite universities for white students as an act of white privilege which is used to enhance their own position of elitism to maintain their power. Consequently, such universities work to maintain and reinforce their representation as white middle-class institutions, reserved for white middle-class students. Black, Pakistani and Bangladeshi groups are less likely than white students to be offered places for entrance into elite Russell Group universities,[28] 'research has also shown that Black, Pakistani and Bangladeshi applicants to Russell Group and other highly selective universities are substantially less likely to be offered places even when they have the same "A" level[29] grades as their white peers'.[30]

Boliver[31] suggests that this may be due to processes of unconscious bias. The application process for admission to universities entails admissions officers receiving non-anonymised applications which include the name of applicants and other details. Their ethnicity is not included at this stage but is revealed after a decision has been made. Boliver suggests that '[t]he possibility of direct discrimination, perhaps resulting from unconscious bias cannot be ruled out'.[32]

Other research suggests that it is not just elite Russell Group universities that are rejecting black and minority ethnic applicants. Noden et al[33] found that offer rates for those from black and minority ethnic backgrounds were lower than those for whites when applying for Russell Group, traditional red brick, and new universities (even after controlling for 'A' level grades). 'For example, compared to White applicants who are equally well qualified at "A" level, Black Caribbean applicants have a seven percentage points lower offer rate from Russell Group universities, and a four percentage points lower offer rate from both old and new universities'.[34]

In October 2015, then Prime Minister David Cameron proposed to introduce 'name-blind' applications for the Universities and Colleges Admissions System (UCAS) forms for applications to universities in an attempt to tackle unconscious bias used in application procedures, aiming for a 20% increase in the numbers of black and minority ethnic students attending university by 2020.[35] There are currently four universities participating in a trial of name-blind UCAS applications: Exeter, Liverpool, Huddersfield and Winchester.[36] However, it is unlikely that all universities will adopt the name-blind process from 2017. After a consultation process UCAS concluded that '… there is insufficient evidence of a problem to warrant the scale of investment and business change that would be needed to adopt name-blind applications'.[37]

Out of place?

Inequalities in admissions processes as evidenced above suggest that universities remain white middle-class spaces. They require students to adopt particular ways of *being* and *doing* – those which conform to middle-class practices that define success in higher education: ways of writing, speaking and the use of academic language. Universities measure a particular type of success that is possessed by those from white middle-class backgrounds. The lack of identity with academic life can impact negatively on students who feel out of place in a white middle-class environment. 'Students from under-represented backgrounds often experience feelings of unworthiness or shame, which are related to processes of misrecognition'.[38] Burke suggests that '[i]nclusion tends to be more about fitting into the dominant culture than about interrogating that culture for the ways that it is complicit in the social and cultural reproduction of exclusion, misrecognition and inequality'.[39]

Universities have particular norms of behaviour that are racialised and divided by class, as well as ethnicity. Burke suggests that

> [a]n ethical framework for widening participation requires universities to provide the resources and opportunities for students from under-represented backgrounds to develop their understanding of ways of writing, reading, speaking and learning that will

facilitate their access to privileged forms of being and knowing, whilst at the same time encouraging spaces of change and transformation.[40]

A recent report published by the National Union of Students[41] found that many black students felt rejected and let down by the higher education system. Some of the key issues students spoke about were the Eurocentric curriculum, which black students felt they could not relate to, biased marking, hate crime on campus and the lack of black academics as role models, which affected their marginal status in the white space of the academy. As a result of this marginalisation, mentoring schemes to tackle these issues have been developed in some universities. These schemes suggest that black students should be encouraged to discuss their experiences of racism in specific safe spaces in which they should not be made to feel like the 'problem'; instead the structure of the academy needs to be addressed and challenged.[42]

Racism and racist practices dominate the experiences of black and minority students in higher education. Bouattia suggests that '[t]he conversation has been considerably watered down to the extent that the use of terms like "racism" or even "discrimination" to describe student experiences are rarely uttered and the HE [higher education] sector and institutions [are] rarely criticised let alone held accountable for what Black students are facing'.[43]

Universities must listen to and address the challenges that black and minority ethnic students face in higher education. There is ample evidence to suggest that black and minority ethnic students remain marginalised and disadvantaged in higher education, yet few universities have policies and strategies in place to address this. Universities must address the fact that racism takes place in their institutions and exists as part of the social structure of their organisations, and they must move away from a deficit model which blames individuals. Loke suggests that

> [f]or too long, actions have taken a deficit model approach, which presumes the issues are rooted within individual minority ethnic staff and students, rather than within institutional culture. With this

approach, there is an assumption it is cheaper, quicker and easier to think about changing minority ethnic individuals, rather than effecting change across the whole institution.[44]

Postgraduate students

In the last 20 years there has been an increase in the overall numbers of students who participate in postgraduate study, however these figures vary by postgraduate taught courses (Masters) and postgraduate research (MPhil and PhD courses).[45] There has been a significant decrease in the numbers of part-time students and those taking STEMM subjects.[46] The main reason cited for this decline is the lack of funding available to students when they decide to embark on postgraduate study.[47] There is little research that has explored the postgraduate experience. The research that does exist records and assesses postgraduate experiences at the end of courses, rather than before or during.[48]

A recent report published by HEFCE (Higher Education Funding Council for England)[49] explores transitions from first degree qualification to postgraduate study. The report analyses postgraduate enrolment and trends across one-year, three-year and five-year transitions. What is interesting about the report is that it explores the route taken to *reach* graduates' highest level of postgraduate study. The report suggests that transitions to postgraduate study have fallen over the last decade, although transition to postgraduate taught courses has shown a slight increase. Disadvantaged students are less likely to continue to postgraduate study.[50] Black and minority ethnic graduates are more likely than white graduates[51] to go on to postgraduate taught degrees immediately after graduating, and they are also more likely to return to postgraduate taught study after they have had a break. The difference between black and minority ethnic and white groups has narrowed over time. However, black and minority ethnic students are less likely than white students to enter into postgraduate research (PhDs) than white students. This is also true even when students have had a break in their study and when they have taken different routes for postgraduate research study.

Even though black and minority ethnic students are more likely than white students to make the transition to postgraduate taught study, they are less likely to make the transition from postgraduate taught to postgraduate research study. One of the reasons for this may be access to funding. Fees for postgraduate research degrees are approximately £9,250 a year for full-time UK students and £4,625 a year for part-time UK students, and double for international students. Given the lack of funding and scholarships available for postgraduate research degrees, it is hardly surprising that those from black and minority ethnic backgrounds are less likely to be able to pursue PhD study. There is little research that has explored these issues, but there is some evidence to suggest that black and minority ethnic students lack the financial capital needed to progress to postgraduate research study, which has implications for their transition into the labour market and their positions within it.[52]

The Higher Education Statistics Agency (HESA) suggest that '[w]hile BME students continued to have a higher rate of transition to post graduate taught [sic], the difference in transition rates between white and BME (Black and minority ethnic) students transitioning to post graduate taught study significantly decreased across the time series'.[53]

The *Times Higher Education* states:

2.4 per cent of white students had started a degree within five years of graduation, compared with only 1.3% of their peers from ethnic minorities. The gap grows over the five year period, but it is already evident within one year of graduation: 7.1% of ethnic minority graduates who finished their course in 2013–14 were straight into a master's compared with 6.3% of their white classmates. White graduates however, were nearly twice as likely to go directly on to a research degree (1.7% compared with 1%).[54]

Challenging whiteness?

Various campaigns have been set up to challenge the white academy and racism within it, mostly by student activists. In the UK, the 'Why is my Curriculum white?' campaign was set up in 2015 at University College London. This was a response to a white, Eurocentric curriculum in which students challenged the lack of diversity on their courses and reading lists, arguing that the education at universities is shaped by acts of colonialism and imperialism in which the experiences and contributions of non-white groups are ignored.[55] Similar protests have been set up internationally such as the 'Rhodes Must Fall' and 'Decolonise Education' campaigns. The 'Rhodes Must Fall' campaign began in March 2015 in Cape Town, where students protested against the statue of Cecil Rhodes, which was removed a month after the campaign. Protests later followed for the removal of the statue of Cecil Rhodes at Oxford University. The statue stands in Oriel college as a mark of acknowledgement based on the donation he made to the university of £100,000. But it was what Cecil Rhodes represented that was seen as the problem: a divided society in which those from privileged backgrounds are able to prosper and in which whiteness predominates and works to secure and strengthen that privilege.[56]

Higher education in the US

Recent data released by the National Centre for Education Statistics in the US (May 2016) indicates that there were a total of 17.3 million undergraduate students attending universities (or equivalent degree-awarding institutions) and 2.9 million postgraduate students attending universities (or equivalent) in 2014.[57] Figure 6.1 demonstrates that attendance varies by ethnic group. A total of 66% of undergraduate students (both full- and part-time) attended private non-profit institutions in 2014 (for four-year degrees), higher than the number who attended public institutions. A higher percentage of the students at private for-profit institutions were black (29%) than at private non-profit institutions (13%). A higher percentage of the students at public and private for-profit institutions were Hispanic (16% and 15%) than at private non-profit institutions (11%).[58]

Figure 6.1: Percentage distribution of US-resident undergraduate enrolment in degree-granting postsecondary institutions, by institutional level and control and student race/ethnicity: Fall 2014

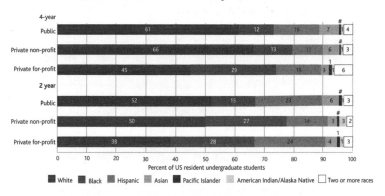

Notes: # Rounds to zero.
Degree-granting Institutions grant associate's or higher degrees and participate in Title IV federal financial aid programmes. Race categories exclude persons of Hispanic ethnicity.

Source: US Department of Education, National Centre for Education Statistics, Integrated Postsecondary Education Data System (IPEDS), Spring 2014, Fall enrolment component.

Figure 6.2 demonstrates that 69% of students attending public institutions were white, compared with 66% at private non-profit and 46% at private for-profit institutions. A total of 36% of black students were attending private for-profit institutions compared with 13% at private non-profit and 11% at public institutions. However, Hispanic students accounted for 9% of graduates across the different types of institutions.[59]

Recent statistics suggest that there has been an increase in the numbers of minority black and ethnic groups attending universities in the US. In 2014 a total of 17.3 million undergraduate students were attending university; of these 9.6 million were white, 3.0 million were Hispanic, 2.4 million were black, 1.0 million were Asian, 0.1 million were American

Indian/Alaska Native and 0.1 million were Pacific Islander. Between 2000 and 2014 there was an increase in the numbers of Hispanic students attending university (the numbers more than doubled from 1.4 to 3.0 million). Those attending from black backgrounds also increased by 57% (from 1.5 million to 2.4 million) and the participation of white students increased by 7% (9.0 million to 9.6 million).[60]

Figure 6.2: Percentage distribution of US-resident post-baccalaureate enrolment in degree-granting postsecondary institutions, by institutional control and student race/ethnicity: Fall 2014

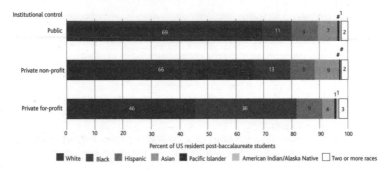

Notes: # Rounds to zero.
Degree-granting institutions grant associate's or higher degrees and participate in Title IV federal financial aid programmes. Race categories exclude persons of Hispanic ethnicity.

Source: US Department of Education, National Centre for Education Statistics, Integrated Postsecondary Education Data System (IPEDS), Spring 2015, Fall enrolment component. See *Digest of Education Statistics 2015*, table 306.50.

For Masters and Doctoral programmes 2.9 million students enrolled on these courses in 2014; of these the majority were white (1,656,000), 336,000 were black, 230,000 were Hispanic, 191,000 were Asian, 14,000 were American Indian/Alaska native and 7,000 were Pacific Islander. During 2000–2014 the number of black and Hispanic students enrolled on postgraduate courses more than doubled, the numbers of black students increased from 181,000 to 366,000 and Hispanic from 111,000 to 230,000 students.[61]

In the US, academic success is often attributed to access to social mobility and the belief in a meritocracy. Gaining access to a good college and a high-ranking university is understood to be part of a meritocratic society in which those who are competent, able and intelligent are rewarded for their efforts. However, such a system continues to privilege the few.[62] Access to such privilege is related to the possession of cultural and social capital, which enables the formation of social networks to reinforce those already in privileged positions to maintain, perpetuate and pass on these privileges to their children. But, does higher education simply reproduce this privilege? Karabel, when examining admissions to elite universities such as Harvard, Princeton and Yale, argues that '[t]he definition of "merit" is fluid and tends to reflect the values and interests of those in power to impose their particular cultural ideals'.[63] In the US, racial diversity is considered one of the defining features of a university, particularly in relation to positioning in league tables.[64]

Affirmative action

Affirmative action has been in existence in the US since the 1960s and is based on a set of laws, policies and guidelines to be implemented in organisations to counter discrimination based on race and gender. Many selective private universities and public universities use affirmative action (though there has been a ban in some states). Research suggests positive benefits for all students when affirmative action is used. Warikoo argues that '... there are academic and civil benefits to racial diversity on campus, showing that cross-racial interactions are associated with increased self reported intellectual abilities, increased self-reported ability to get along with other race groups, increased interest in promoting racial understanding, and reduced inter group prejudice for students of all racial backgrounds'.[65]

However racism continues to dominate US society. For example, there is ample evidence to suggest that white Americans hold overtly racist views towards minority ethnic groups in the US.[66] White Americans show particularly negative attitudes towards affirmative action,[67] with many seeing it as rewarding black African Americans for negative cultural characteristics[68] (such as stereotypes of black African Americans as being drug takers and violent aggressors and living off welfare). Yet there is evidence to suggest that the main beneficiaries of affirmative action are white women (see Chapter Three for further discussion on this).

One of the ways in which universities in the US show their commitment to diversity and equity is by providing students with an inclusive curriculum. Affirmative action in the 1960s led to the introduction of African American departments which offered degrees on black history and culture. Many universities introduced departments which specifically addressed diversity and equity. However, the mere existence of such programmes and departments does not demonstrate that issues of race and diversity are being dealt with. The existence of such initiatives does not address the power inequalities between white and black groups that continue to exist on campuses in the US – and indeed the rest of society.

On the surface, universities give the impression of 'doing diversity' but such initiatives may cause resentment from white groups towards those from black and minority ethnic backgrounds who are perceived as being given special treatment because of their race. Kinder and Sanders define racial resentment as '... a contemporary expression of racial discord' that 'features indignation as a central emotional theme, one provoked by the sense that black Americans are getting and taking more than their fair share'.[69] Consequently, white groups are less likely to support affirmative action if they think that they as white people will be disadvantaged by it.[70] White groups are more likely to see affirmative action as a trade-off, which in theory they support – as long as it does not disadvantage them or threaten their own position. When this takes place in higher education it is what Warikoo calls a 'diversity bargain'. 'Under-represented minority students can be admitted under affirmative action with lower ... scores as long as those students then contribute to the educational experiences of their peers by not getting rewards "over" white peers and by integrating so that collective merit of the cohort can enrich everyone's education'.[71] She states:

To many white students, minority students do not hold up their end of the diversity bargain when they join the Black Students Association or sit together in the cafeteria. More abstractly, students can feel the diversity bargain has not been upheld by institutions when they lose out in a competitive process such as college admission, applying for an internship or job, or more.[72]

There is a belief that many white students who attend elite institutions feel they have earned their place, rather than inherited it, despite the wealth of evidence which suggests that this is not the case. Furthermore, '... the focus on personal benefits of affirmative action in contrast to a more compensatory goal ignores the historical and structural discrimination that continues to affect racial minorities today and suggests that racial inequality and discrimination are no longer significant'.[73]

Black and Latino young people continue to be under-represented at Harvard and Brown and other selective universities in the US.[74] The evidence points to the existence of racial inequalities in higher education in the US. Whiteness and white privilege dominate to maintain and reinforce the whiteness of higher education institutions. This can be viewed as a colour-blind perspective in which many white people ignore the role that their own racial privilege, that of whiteness, plays in a system from which they continue to benefit. Their own privilege of whiteness dictates that they fail to see how they benefit from their own white identity and white privilege.[75]

There is a belief that racism exists as a result of the individual acts of a small number of people. This view is often held by whites, yet the evidence points to many structural disadvantages that black groups face in America – in schools, universities and the labour market, as well as in relation to poverty and crime. There is a plethora of evidence to suggest that black groups continue to experience institutional racism in all areas of society (as discussed above). Bonilla-Silva suggests that this perspective is based on a system of 'racism without racists' in which whites perpetuate 'white supremacy' as 'social relations and practices that reinforce white privilege'.[76] From this perspective, '[w]hites' emphasis on colour-blindness in the analysis of inequality legitimates white privilege, consequently denying the importance of social policies to ameliorate black disadvantage'.[77]

Whiteness in higher education operates as a form of legitimacy, by which white students who attend elite universities maintain their position of advantage by defending the legitimacy of the system that has led to their advantageous position within it. This is based on white groups privileging their individual rights over those of others.[78] As a result, elite universities maintain their privileges by reinforcing white privilege. Consequently, black, Latino and working-class poor students continue to be vastly under-represented at elite universities in the US.[79] There is also evidence to suggest that inequalities in admissions processes for non-white groups to selective universities are increasing rather than decreasing,[80] and the percentage of black students who attend selective universities showed a decrease rather than an increase from 1982 to 2004.[81] White students are able to legitimise and justify their attendance at elite universities because they believe that it is a meritocracy that enabled them to be there, rather than their white privilege, their class and/or their social connections.[82]

Universities reinforce, protect and perpetuate their elite identity with which they justify their position of superiority. As long as white identity and white privilege are not threatened, white groups are supportive of diversity and inclusion programmes such as affirmative action. Consequently, universities can sell themselves as diverse and fair as long as their white privilege remains intact and unthreatened.

Conclusions

In this chapter I have argued that while the numbers of students from minority ethnic backgrounds attending university has shown a steady increase in the last decade, inequalities in higher education continue to persist in the UK and the US. The brightest non-white students are still less likely than their white peers to attend elite universities. Universities are key spaces in which whiteness and white identities predominate. This is not just in the representation of white groups occupying decision-making senior roles, it is also evidenced in the curriculum and approaches to diversity, inclusion and social justice. Far from being liberal spaces of inclusion, higher education institutions continue to perpetuate the superiority and predominance of whiteness and as a result universities remain spaces reserved for the privileged few.

Elite universities are the epitome of the legitimation and reproduction of institutional racism. They continue to play their part in the reproduction and reinforcement of racial and class inequalities. In this system of exclusion, black and minority ethnic students remain marginalised and excluded. Higher education institutions are spaces of white privilege which fail to cater for the experiences of black and minority ethnic groups. They employ a rhetoric of inclusion, but one that is rarely evidenced in practice or outcomes.

SEVEN

Racism and bullying in the UK

This chapter will explore how equality policies operate to regulate public behaviour but in which racist behaviours are unacknowledged. The chapter will draw on two UK case studies, one exploring parents' complaints about racism in schools and the other focussing on racism experienced by black and minority ethnic academics in higher education. The chapter will argue that whiteness and white identities are protected when complaints of racism are made. It will examine how recent policy developments such as the Equality Act 2010, in its attempts to protect individuals from discrimination, marginalises those from black and minority ethnic backgrounds. When complaints about racism are made, policies and attitudes within schools and universities fail to acknowledge the existence of such behaviour. As a result, a failure to acknowledge racist acts works to protect white identities and dismiss acts of racism.

Bullying in schools

In the UK there is a legal requirement for all state schools to have behaviour policies in place to encourage positive behaviour in schools. Section 89 of the Education and Inspections Act 2006 specifies that maintained schools must have specific measures in place which encourage good behaviour and prevent all forms of bullying among pupils. All schools should have behaviour policies in place in which the prevention of bullying must be communicated to pupils, staff and parents.

Schools are also expected to abide by the Equality Act 2010 (see Chapter Six for a detailed discussion of the Equality Act and its workings). Part 6 of the Equality Act refers to bullying and what schools must do to address this. The Department for Education (DfE) states:

> Part 6 of the Act makes it unlawful for the responsible body of a school to discriminate against, harass or victimise a pupil or potential pupil in relation to admissions, the way it provides education for pupils, provision of pupil access to any benefit, facility or service, or by excluding a pupil or subjecting them to any other detriment.[1]

The DfE guidelines also suggest that under the Children Act 1989 bullying should be addressed as an issue of child protection when there is 'reasonable cause to suspect that a child is suffering or is likely to suffer significant harm'.[2] If this happens, it is the school's responsibility to report such concerns to the local authority. The DfE suggest that '[e]ven where safeguarding is not considered to be an issue, schools may need to draw on a range of external services to support the pupil who is experiencing bullying, or to tackle any underlying issue which has contributed to a child engaging in bullying'.[3]

All schools are expected to have active measures in place to be able to deal with bullying and create an environment in which bullying is not tolerated.

> A school's response to bullying should not start at the point at which a child has been bullied. The best schools develop a more sophisticated approach in which school staff proactively gather intelligence about issues between pupils which might provoke conflict and develop strategies to prevent bullying occurring in the first place.[4]

A holistic approach must be taken to address bullying. Successful schools that are able to tackle bullying involve parents, pupils, implement disciplinary sanctions, use specific organisations for support, develop an inclusive culture, make it easy to report bullying and provide effective staff training to deal with bullying.[5]

While there are clear guidelines on behaviour policies, the DfE does not provide a single definition of bullying. Each school has its own definition. The DfE defines it as repeated behaviour that is

> intended to hurt someone either physically or emotionally, often aimed at certain groups (because of their race, religion, gender or sexual orientation). It may take many forms and can include physical assault, teasing, making threats, name calling, cyber bullying (bullying via mobile phone or online such as email, social networks and instant messenger).[6]

In 2012, a total of 88,000 racist incidents were recorded in British schools between 2004 and 2011. Data collected from 90 areas in the UK found that 87,915 cases of racist bullying were reported to schools, which included name calling and physical abuse.[7] Under the Race Relations (Amendment) Act 2000, after the publication of the Sir William Macpherson report, schools had a statutory duty to record and report all racist incidents to their local authorities in order that racism could be monitored, measured and acted on. The Race Relations (Amendment) Act 2000 made racial discrimination an unacceptable offence and imposed a general duty on public bodies to ensure that they were promoting racial equality and positive relations between people from different minority ethnic backgrounds. Public bodies were expected to be proactive in promoting positive relationships in their organisations and assess their policies and procedures in relation to race, in order that the implementation of policies could be monitored on a regular basis.

However since the Coalition Government of 2010–2015, the specific duties placed on schools in their obligation to report and monitor racist incidents have been scrapped and schools are no longer required by law to record or report any incidents of racism or racist behaviour. Data suggests that just before the legal requirement was scrapped, racist incidents increased. 'Between 2007 and 2010 – the last year that heads had an obligation to record cases – recorded racist incidents in schools in England, Scotland and Wales rose from 22,285 to 23,971'.[8] However, these figures may be the tip of the iceberg, with many children afraid to report racism for fear of it not being taken seriously or fear of reprisals.[9]

While the Equality Act requires all schools to have bullying policies in place, the Coalition Government strategy significantly weakened the specific duties required under the Equality Act. 'The new duties only place two obligations on public authorities: a need to publish equality information about service users and the workforce (if there are over 150 employees) and a need to publish "at least one" equality objective'.[10] Compliance with the new duties did not come into effect until 31 January 2012 for public bodies, and 6 April 2012 for schools. The Trades Union Congress (TUC) suggested that the Coalition Government introduce a 'light touch' approach to equality issues. Writing in 2013 they argued that '[r]ecent statements from coalition government ministers show a lack of leadership in driving change and a failure to recognise the importance of good quality information on equality for policy formation and progress monitoring'.[11] Furthermore, this signifies that the monitoring of race equality is seen as insignificant. Such an approach led by the Coalition Government further undermined the importance of equity and a social justice agenda. The TUC suggests that such attacks threatened the aims of equality taking a front seat by

> placing more obstacles in the way of those trying to bring about positive change within public sector organisations and making it harder for stakeholders to use the duty to press for action. This is at a time when many of those individuals whom the duty was intended to assist are being disproportionately hit by public service cuts and job losses.[12]

Much of the increase in racist bullying has centred on the media rhetoric of immigration and the current refugee crisis in Europe. This is also evidenced in an increase in the numbers of racist incidents reported post-Brexit (see Chapter Two). In 2013 more than 1,400 children contacted ChildLine for counselling specifically about racist bullying. Much of the reporting focussed on racism and Islamophobia, with many young Muslim students reporting being called 'terrorists' and 'bombers' by their peers.[13]

The National Society for the Prevention of Cruelty to Children (NSPCC) suggests that there has been an increase in the numbers of children who are experiencing bullying. In 2015 the NSPCC held 25,700 ChildLine counselling sessions with children specifically about bullying and more than 16,000 children were absent from school because of bullying.[14] In 2016 figures suggested that as many as 20 children per day were excluded due to incidents of racist abuse towards peers. A total of 4,000 cases of racial abuse among school children were seen as being serious enough for schools to impose a fixed or permanent exclusion.[15]

Bullying in higher education institutions

While there is ample evidence to suggest that racist bullying in schools is on the increase, there is also a plethora of evidence to suggest that racism and racist practices continue to exist in higher education institutions. On the one hand, universities are bastions of equality and diversity, liberal institutions at the forefront of instigating change in their contribution to knowledge and adding to the experiences of their students. Yet on the other hand, they continue to be dominated by those from white middle-class backgrounds. The latest figures suggest that if you are from a black or minority ethnic background you are less likely to be in a senior managerial or professorial post in higher education. The Equality Challenge Unit (ECU) states: 'The proportions of UK staff who were BME were markedly below average in senior contract levels above professorial level. For instance between 2014-2015 among UK staff 3.4% of deputy/pro-vice chancellors, 2.1% of chief operating officers/registrars/university secretaries and none of the 130 UK national heads of institutions were BME'. In 2014-2015 a higher proportion of white academic staff (31.3%) earned more than £50,000 compared with UK black and minority ethnic staff (28.9%). In the same period in terms of professional and support staff, white staff were more likely to earn £30,000 and over (35.1%)

compared with 34.4% of UK black and minority ethnic staff.[16] Furthermore, there are only three vice chancellors in the UK who are from a black or minority ethnic background (Valerie Amos, SOAS; former Labour Cabinet Minister, Gerald Pillay of Liverpool Hope University, who was born in South Africa but is of Indian descent; and Rama Thirunamachandran of Canterbury Christ Church University, who is of Sri Lankan origin).[17]

There is evidence to suggest that racism persists in higher education institutions. A recent report carried out by the University and College Union (UCU), which focussed specifically on the experiences of black academics in higher education, found racism was commonplace for the majority of academics working in colleges and universities.

> Respondents were asked to think about scenarios at work and rate associated statements in accordance with their own experiences. Those scenarios and statements related to their personal experiences of progression and promotion, if they perceived they have been on the receiving end of bullying, their sense of inclusion or exclusion in decision-making processes and whether they had been subject to cultural insensitivity.[18]

The UCU research was based on a total of 631 UCU black members, of whom 446 were working in higher education institutions and 185 were working in further education. The survey covered different areas such as promotion and progress; experiences of bullying; participation in decision-making; and issues of cultural sensitivity. The majority of respondents working in higher education (90%) and further education (88%) said they had experienced barriers to promotion. Furthermore, the majority of respondents working in higher education (59%) and further education (58%) did not feel they were supported in seeking promotion or progression.[19]

The majority of respondents working in higher education (72%) institutions and in further education (70%) felt they had experienced some form of bullying and harassment from managers. This was also the case in relation to experiencing bullying and harassment from colleagues (69% of respondents working in higher education institutions and 67% working in further education). Respondents also felt they were subjected to cultural insensitivity (85% of those working in higher education and 73% working in further education).

UCU argue that their survey

> suggests that racism is present in our colleges and universities. It warns that there is a persistent glass ceiling for black employees across post-16 education and also that too many have experienced bullying at work. They have also found themselves excluded from decision-making and subject to cultural sensitivity. According to this survey, the barriers to progression are stronger in higher education than in further education.[20]

Black staff also said they faced isolation and lack of support when they experienced bullying and harassment at work. The UCU research suggests that when individuals raise concerns about racism, this leads to further isolation. Significant changes must be made, particularly at senior decision-making levels. 'Leadership in colleges and universities must be prepared to radically examine their structures, policies and procedures – in essence change the organisational structure and stop paying "lip service" to challenging racism at the expense of black workers'.[21]

A recent report published by the ECU[22] found that black and minority ethnic academics are more likely to consider a move overseas compared with their white colleagues. Many respondents in the ECU study wanted universities to take specific direct action regarding the inclusion of black and minority ethnic staff in higher education. This was based on representation and inclusivity of black and minority ethnic culture in higher education. The ECU states that 'Respondents provided examples of inappropriate behaviour from their colleagues which highlighted both a lack of awareness that the behaviour was offensive and covert and subtle forms of racism. Respondents noted that it was difficult to challenge such behaviours and/or to report them anywhere'.[23]

The research cited above suggests evidence to demonstrate that racism and racist bullying remain key issues in higher education, yet this type of behaviour continues to persist. Despite significant policy changes (such as the Equality Act and the introduction of the recent Race Equality Charter), inequalities and processes of exclusion continue to occur in higher education and schools.

Evidence also suggests that students are more likely to have racist, biased attitudes towards lecturers who are from black and minority ethnic backgrounds. Recent research based on an analysis of the National Student Survey[24] found that black and minority ethnic academics were more likely to receive lower teaching scores and negative feedback from students compared with their white colleagues. The National Student Survey is a major census of students across the UK, based on the experiences of students in the final year of their undergraduate degree. It is used to measure the success of a university and influences league table results. It is also accessed by parents when selecting universities for their children.

Bell and Brooks[25] suggest that processes of unconscious bias are apparent in students' reporting. They compared National Student Survey results with data from the Higher Education Statistics Agency (HESA) and concluded that for each 1% rise in the number of academic staff who are white, there was an equivalent 0.06% increase in student satisfaction. Ethnicity of lecturers had the second most significant effect on the results as a whole, when compared with other variables. The report suggests that '… overall students are happiest when taught by staff with the following characteristics: white, full professors, and holding doctorates'.[26] Such findings suggest that unconscious bias towards black and minority ethnic staff could affect league table results, as well as individual academic career trajectories. Such findings may affect staff recruitment processes, in which some universities may be reluctant to employ individuals from black and minority ethnic backgrounds.[27] There is similar evidence to suggest that non-white academics are judged more harshly in the US, based on comments posted on the *Rate My Professor* website.[28]

There is often a denial of the existence of racism in the liberal academy. A failure to acknowledge racism results in universities failing to address it. Legislation such as the Equality Act is in place to identify and address different types of discrimination such as racism but provides little information on how to specifically *address* such discrimination. In the two following case studies I demonstrate how legislation such as the Equality Act 2010 works to control and regulate public behaviour in which racism manifests in covert, subtle and nuanced ways.

MR AND MRS BROWN

Mr and Mrs Brown and their children live in a semi-rural village on the outskirts of a small town on the south coast of England. They previously lived in a large city and moved to the south coast when Mr Brown secured a job as a consultant in the local hospital. Mrs Brown was an accountant but gave up working when she gave birth to her third child. Mr and Mrs Brown describe themselves as black Caribbean British. Both their parents were originally from Jamaica and Mr and Mrs Brown were both born in the UK. They have three children: Sam the oldest is 10, Jack is seven and Julie the youngest is five. Mr and Mrs Brown live in a relatively affluent village. Their children attend the local primary school, which was graded 'outstanding' in the most recent OFSTED[29] inspection. The village is predominantly white, with only two other families from black and minority ethnic backgrounds living there.

Sam is a shy, quiet child and when he first started school he struggled to make friends. During that time, he was picked on by one child. Mrs Brown became worried about this.

> 'I did speak to the head teacher and told her that the boy was always doing things to make Sam feel bad, he would put him down and pick on him. It made Sam feel that he was sometimes worried about play times because that was when it happened.'

After having spoken to the head teacher the behaviour stopped but after three months the bullying started again and this time it took on a racist element.

> 'Sam came home one day very upset and said that X – along with others – started to say things to him, like we don't like blacks in

our school, you're black so get out of our school. There were lots of things that were said. And it sounded to me like they were all ganging up on Sam and most of this happened when they were on a coach back from a school trip.'

Mr and Mrs Brown went to see the head teacher and were shocked by her initial response.

'She denied it all and said that these things were not said. She then turned it on Sam and tried to say it was all his fault. She started to bring up the fact that when he first started he couldn't make friends and that maybe it was his personality and the way he behaved that made others react to him.'

Clearly the Browns were very upset by this. The head teacher also insinuated that they had complained several times before and their complaints were unfounded. The Browns felt that they were being victimised for complaining.

'She then went on to say that we had complained in the past about several things and made it sound like we were just complaining for the sake of it. It was as if she was blaming us and we felt bad that we had made a complaint in the first place. We felt we were being told off for making a complaint.'

After several attempts at speaking to the head teacher and her failure to acknowledge and act on the complaints, Mr and Mrs Brown decided to make a formal complaint to the Director of Education. Due to the Smith's persistence, the local authority decided to investigate the case and the teachers, the Browns and some of the children were interviewed in the process of the investigation. The local authority concluded that no evidence of racism or discrimination was found.

'I knew that this would be the outcome, because how are they going to find evidence that it was racism? The boys aren't going to say they called Sam a blackie are they? They aren't going to say that they said all blacks are dirty that's why they have black skin and they aren't going to say that they said blacks should go back and live with other blacks. I knew what the outcome would be, it would always come down on the side of the school and the head teacher. But we had to make a point so that other people could think about it, and that these things do happen and they do go on.'

After the complaint Mr and Mrs Brown decided to take their children out of the school and sent them to a neighbouring school. The incident continues to upset the family.

'It was the fact that it wasn't taken seriously in the first place and that the head teacher wouldn't even think racism could happen in her school. That was the most upsetting thing. We were made to look like we were just causing trouble and that we were making it all up. Why would we want to do this? It has caused our family a lot of stress and disrupted the children's education.'

A failure on the school's part to acknowledge that racism had taken place was followed by a failure to address ways of moving forward. By making a complaint, the Browns, who were the victims of racism, became the villains – simply *because* they had made a complaint about racism. Because they had made complaints in the past, they were labelled as 'troublemakers' who lacked credibility. Their non-white identity positioned them as 'others' who were outside the normality of whiteness. A refusal to address racism resulted in a desire to protect whiteness and white privilege. Mr and Mrs Brown were also adamant that the school did not follow the correct procedures when the bullying took place.

'I looked at their bullying policy and it was not followed and they have nothing at all on race at the school but they do in the county council and I had a look at that policy. But it's designed in such a way that you have to have someone call you a racist name for it to be addressed. It seems that these policies are in place for the sake of having a policy, but if you make a complaint they're designed so that it's never going to be shown to be proven. So the victims will lose out whatever happens, you make a complaint and the process is about proving it did *not* happen, rather than finding the evidence that it *did*.'

The mere existence of policy making does not indicate that inequality is being addressed, instead such policies work to curb public behaviour and present an illusion that issues are being dealt with. When Mr and Mrs Brown made a complaint, their complaint was not taken at face value. An assumption was made that the complaint was false and that the incident did not take place. By making a complaint, Mr and Mrs Brown became the villains, rather than the victims of racism. Through such a process, whiteness and white privilege operated to reinforce and marginalise the 'other'.

KULDEEP

Kuldeep was a Reader in a Russell Group university. She had been a Reader for five years when a white female member of staff joined also as a Reader in her department. It was after Kuldeep returned from study leave that she noticed that her colleague began belittling her in public and constantly criticising her.

> 'She suddenly became very hostile towards me, I'm not sure what it was all about. But she would make comments about the way I looked – trying to be funny and then would try and do anything to catch me out. In meetings she would also pick out something negative and use that against me. This went on for a long time and was very upsetting.'

Kuldeep spoke to her manager, indicating that she felt that she was being bullied and that she felt the bullying may have a racial element. But her manager said that it was probably just a clash of personalities and that she just didn't get along with her colleague.

> 'He kind of in one way was very sympathetic but in another didn't take it very seriously saying, oh you just don't get on and you clash because of your personalities. It was brushed aside and it was seen as me making a big issue out of something that wasn't there. I think he wanted us to get along and work together but in a way that was his was of dismissing it and then he didn't have to deal with it. It was my problem and not his.'

Kuldeep also noticed that her colleague would often make negative and derogatory comments about students who were from Muslim backgrounds and female students with children.

> 'She said one day that we shouldn't be catering for "those kind of people", they are here and this is the way we do things over here. I was shocked and no one else said anything about it. She would also put the students down who had children and said we cannot provide support for "these people". She didn't have children herself and knew that I had children and that in the past I had asked for a meeting she called at 9am to be moved to 10am and she has held that against me ever since.'

Other examples of her behaviour included ignoring Kuldeep in meetings and making her feel that her opinion was not worthy.

> 'If she was chairing a meeting, she would totally ignore me. Not give me eye contact and ignore any comments I made – or took that opportunity to put me down. Other people began to notice it and said she was behaving in a way which suggested she had a problem with me.'

The racist bullying continued and Kuldeep decided to go and speak to her union. She also spoke to her Dean who suggested she made a complaint.

> 'The union were great, they looked at all the incidents I had documented and they said I had a case and should make a complaint. I was going to but then I knew I was going on study leave again and would wait and see what happened when I returned. Even the Dean said I should make a complaint which was a real surprise to me. I thought she would have wanted me to keep quiet.'

When Kuldeep returned from study leave her colleague had been promoted to a Chair and given a senior role as Director of Research. Kuldeep decided it was time to leave and finally left the university.

There is evidence to suggest that Kuldeep's case is not unique. When complaints about racism are made, the refusal of line managers to take such complaints seriously and simply dismiss them as a 'clash of personalities' suggests a process by which a failure to acknowledge such acts works to protect white identities.

Racist behaviour manifests in subtle, nuanced and covert ways and is dismissed and ignored by senior managers, who fail to take it seriously. The acceptance of covert racism undermines the position of the victim and questions whether such behaviour is genuine. Within the liberal culture of higher education, white privilege is protected and whiteness reinforced within a discourse that fails to recognise or acknowledge racist acts, with a dismissal of such acts simply as a 'clash of personalities'.

The failure of higher education institutions to accept the existence of racism is an example of the perpetuation of white privilege and whiteness in which mechanisms are used to ensure that those from black and minority ethnic groups know their place. When complaints of racism are made, they are not taken at face value. The idea that racism could take place in higher education is related to a refusal to accept its existence, but this narrative also reinforces the difficulties of challenging such behaviour. When complaints about racism are made a performance of non-racist behaviours which mask covert discreet acts of racism takes place in schools and higher education in which senior managers are complicit in encouraging such a culture. Their failure to acknowledge or act on such behaviour is an example of a manifestation and perpetuation of their position of power. Given these roles (as the evidence suggests) are occupied by white groups, this behaviour and these processes work to reinforce and protect white privilege and the continued perpetuation of white domination. This process is one by which white groups actively protect and perpetuate their own position of privilege and the whiteness of institutions. Consequently, '[a]n inevitable cycle of discriminatory practice emerges in which the presence of equality legislation is promoted publicly but discreetly ignored in practice. As a result BME (black and minority ethnic) colleagues are routinely subjected to biases that are condoned and reproduced in the decision making of departmental management'.[30] This is further reinforced in legislation such as the Equality Act:

> In harmonising previous equality legislation, the Equality Act 2010 inadvertently homogenised general characteristics and by doing so the *specificity* of differences (such as race and gender for example) are not addressed by institutions; rather they focus on overarching generic concerns. Consequently, and counterintuitively, in some respects, institutions are freed from adhering to statutory obligations in relation to race.[31]

The case studies reveal that senior managers in schools and the white liberal academy are reluctant to recognise or address racism or other forms of exclusion which work to marginalise black and minority ethnic groups. The failure to acknowledge such behaviour as racist serves to perpetuate the myth that schools and the academy are free from racism. Instead such failures protect white privilege, with white groups maintaining their power and prestige, and in doing so maintaining schools and the academy as white spaces. This results in a discourse and narrative in which a new 'racetalk' has emerged in which white groups work to maintain their own position of power (at all costs) so that white groups avoid *appearing* to be racist. Such 'colour blind racism allows whites to appear "not racist" and preserve their privileged status'.[32] This is further reinforced in the processes by which senior managers try to address issues of inequality, particularly racism. Özbilgin and Tatli suggest:

> individual and institutional actors that occupy a particular field have unequal access to and ownership of power and resources, which constitutes a significant imbalance in the struggle for domination and legitimacy. Thus not all actors in the equality and diversity field had similar levels of power and influence to determine the direction of change in the framing of equality and diversity.[33]

Conclusions

White privilege operates in the protection of white identities when complaints about racism are made in schools and universities. Schools and universities want to portray a whiteness that is desirable, hence an overwhelming need to protect and privilege white identities manifests itself in which acts of racism are either seen as a 'clash of personalities' or it is incomprehensible that they could take place in the confines of an outstanding school or the corridors of the white, liberal academy.

Policy making such as the Equality Act is used to reinforce the privilege of white identity over and above the concerns of racism raised by parents and academics. Such acts reinforce the stability of white privilege and work to perpetuate whiteness. Merely vocalising a complaint about racism in schools and higher education is seen as an attempt to *challenge, disrupt and question* white privilege. Consequently, racial hierarchies are reinforced in which daring to complain about racism, daring to mention that racism takes place in schools and higher education, becomes a threat to the stability, maintenance and reinforcement of white privilege.

In this process, white privilege is protected and those who complain about acts of racism are aggressive, confrontational and overreacting to what is regarded as a 'clash of personalities'. In schools, '[t]he unhealthy dominance of white privilege and white hegemonic institutions has produced a "culture of complacency"; race and racism are understood to be high on public and political agendas, but understood to be irrelevant to the actualities of ... schools'.[34] Consequently, a failure to acknowledge acts of racism results in a failure to address racism. Such a discourse works to protect white identities and perpetuate white privilege in its failure to acknowledge the presence of racism.

EIGHT

Racial inequalities in the labour market

This chapter will explore the position of black and minority ethnic groups in the labour market. It will argue that through a process of racism black and minority ethnic groups are less likely to occupy positions of power in the labour market. The chapter will explore how race works as a disadvantage in the labour market in which black and minority ethnic groups are more likely to be unemployed or in low-paid and insecure employment compared with their white counterparts. The chapter will explore why ethnic inequalities in the labour market have persisted over time and examine why black and minority ethnic groups are on the one hand entering higher education in high numbers, yet on the other continue to experience unemployment and disadvantages in the labour market.

In previous chapters I have discussed the increase in the numbers of black and minority ethnic students entering higher education. However, while this remains the case, black students are less likely to attend elite Russell Group universities and are less likely than white students to leave university with a 2:1 or first-class degree. There is also evidence to suggest inequalities in postgraduate study (postgraduate taught Master's and PhD research). Recent research suggests that while there has been an expansion in postgraduate taught study, there has also been a decline in the numbers of postgraduate-taught student numbers (both UK and overseas students).[1,2,3]

Qualifications obtained at undergraduate and postgraduate level have a direct influence on transitions to the labour market and social mobility within it. If black and minority ethnic students are less likely to enter postgraduate research study, this will have a direct impact on their labour market experiences.

This chapter examines the labour market experiences of black and minority ethnic groups, who find themselves positioned as outsiders in a system that continues to reward white privilege. There is evidence to suggest that inequalities in the labour market are directly related to high levels of poverty experienced by some black and minority ethnic groups.[4] Furthermore, examining the different experiences of black and minority ethnic groups leads us to question whether equality of opportunity is a reality for some and not others.

Labour market participation

There has been a wealth of evidence to suggest that historically those from black and minority ethnic groups are less likely to be economically active compared with white groups. Recent evidence continues to point towards this trend, with some changes for some minority ethnic groups. In a recent analysis of 2011 census data by the Office for National Statistics (ONS)[5] using the Labour Force Survey statistics, the evidence suggests that employment rates for those from black and minority ethnic groups continue to be lower than those from white groups. For example, in 2014, the white group were more likely than any other group to have the highest level of employment (75%) compared with all other ethnic groups. White employment has consistently tended to be at least 10% higher than all non-white groups.

Those from black and minority ethnic groups are also more likely to be economically inactive compared with white groups. In 2014 a total of 21% of the white group were economically inactive, compared with 28% of black and 32% of Asian groups.[6]

There is also variation *across* ethnic groups and labour market participation. The white population has the highest employment rate of all ethnic groups with 73% of white British people in employment. Other ethnic groups are less likely to be in employment including all black (61%) and Asian (60%) groups; within these categories there are even starker indications of inequalities with less than half of Pakistani and Bangladeshi people in employment and only 40% of Gypsies and Travellers.[7]

Figure 8.1: Employment rates by ethnic group, England and Wales

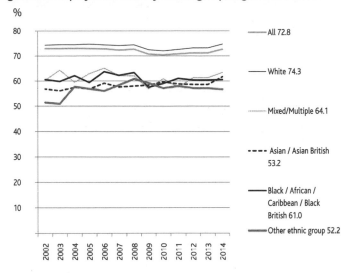

Source: ONS (2012) *A Comparison of the 2011 Census and Labour Force Survey, Labour Market Indicators*, https://tinyurl.com/.

Figure 8.2: Economic inactivity rates by ethnic group, England and Wales, 2001 to 2014 (LFS April to June)

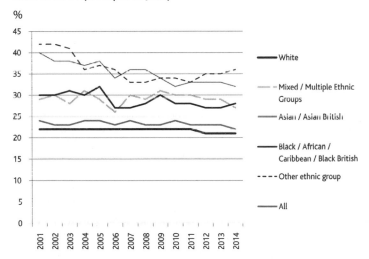

Source: ONS (2012) *A Comparison of the 2011 Census and Labour Force Survey, Labour Market Indicators*, https://tinyurl.com/.

Table 8.1: Economic activity of people aged 16–64, by ethnic group, England and Wales, 2011 Census

Percentages

	In employment	Unemployed	Inactive	Total numbers in thousands ('000')
ALL	71	6	23	36,274
White	73	5	22	31,055
English/Welsh/Scottish/Northern Irish/British	73	5	22	28,732
Irish	73	5	22	338
Gypsy or Irish Traveller	40	10	50	36
Other White	77	5	19	1,949
Mixed/multiple ethnic group	60	11	30	638
White and Black Caribbean	56	14	30	225
White and Black African	59	11	29	81
White and Asian	62	8	31	171
Other Mixed	63	9	29	161
Asian/Asian British	60	7	33	2,937
Indian	70	6	24	1,026
Pakistani	49	9	42	705
Bangladeshi	48	10	41	275
Chinese	53	5	43	323
Other Asian	63	6	31	608
Black/African/Caribbean/Black British	61	13	26	1,241
African	59	13	28	667
Caribbean	67	12	22	408
Other Black	56	14	29	165
Other ethnic group	53	9	39	403
Arab	42	8	50	157
Any other ethnic group	59	9	32	246

Source: Office for National Statistics (ONS, 2014a).

In terms of unemployment, those from white/black Caribbean ethnic groups (both men and women) were more likely to be unemployed. Black African women (12%) and white/black Caribbean (11%) and 'other' black women (11%) were also more likely to be unemployed than other women.[8]

The census data also shows differences by ethnic group and gender in terms of types of employment. For example, while a total of 37% of men in the population work in low-skilled occupations, those from Pakistani (59%), black African (54%) and Bangladeshi backgrounds (53%) are much more likely to be engaged in such employment. Across the whole population, the majority of women (59%) in employment are working in low-skilled occupations. When this is considered by ethnicity, there are still startling discrepancies, with women from Caribbean and Bangladeshi backgrounds more likely to be employed in low-skilled work.[9] There are different reasons and explanations as to why some groups are inactive in the labour market compared with others. The census explanations are based on student activity, long-term sickness or disability, family and domestic responsibilities or retirement.[10]

Figure 8.3: Economic activity for males (aged 16–64) by ethnic group, England and Wales, 2011 Census

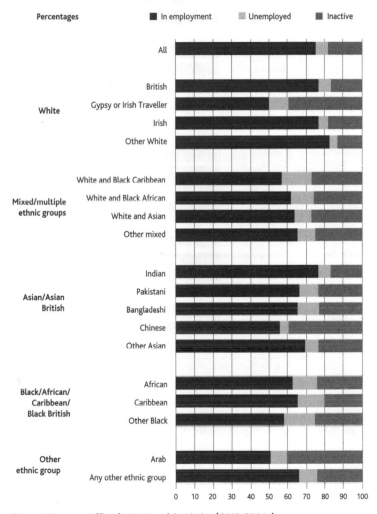

Source: Census – Office for National Statistics (ONS, 2014a).

Figure 8.4: Economic activity for females (aged 16–64) by ethnic group, England and Wales, 2011 Census

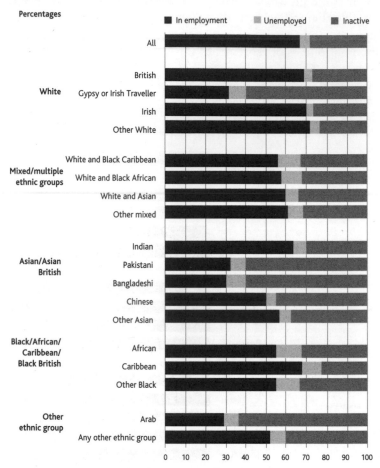

Source: Census – Office for National Statistics, (ONS, 2014a).

Different ethnic groups are concentrated in particular sectors of the labour market. For example, the census data shows that Asian/Asian British men were more likely than other groups to work in the accommodation and food services (such as hotels and restaurants) and wholesale and retail (shops). Women from black and 'other Asian' groups were more likely to be working in the health and social work sector, for example local authority carers.[11]

Figure 8.5: Men and women in low-skilled occupations by ethnic group, England and Wales, 2011 Census

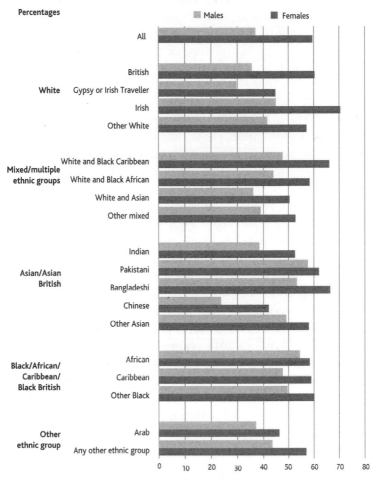

Source. Census – Office for National Statistics, (ONS, 2014a).

Why are there ethnic differences in the labour market?

A recent Equalities and Human Rights Commission (EHRC) report suggests vast disparities in the labour market for those from black and minority ethnic groups.[12] Taken as a whole, unemployment rates across Britain were significantly higher for people from all other ethnic minority backgrounds (12.9%) than those for white people (6.3%) in 2013. White young people are more likely than those from black and minority ethnic backgrounds to gain apprenticeships (89% compared with 2%) and if you are from a black background and you have a degree you will earn 23.1% less on average than if you are from a white background.[13]

Furthermore, 'young ethnic minorities experienced the worst long-term employment outcomes. Between 2010–2015, they saw a 49% rise in unemployment compared with a fall of 1% in overall long-term youth unemployment and a 2% fall among young white people'.[14] Changes in labour market participation suggest a decrease in differences in minority ethnic participation, however those from black backgrounds (both men and women) have experienced the greatest decreases in full-time employment during 2006, 2008 and 2013. Hills et al[15] suggest that this may be a result of the recession and austerity measures introduced from 2010.

There is also evidence to suggest that those from black and Asian backgrounds are more likely to be in insecure forms of employment compared with their white counterparts.[16] For example, they were twice as likely to be in involuntary temporary employment (4.3%) in 2014 compared with those from white backgrounds (2.1%). The Trades Union Congress (TUC)[17] suggests that the numbers of black and Asian workers in insecure forms of employment increased by nearly 40% between 2011 and 2014, compared with a 16% increase for those from white backgrounds.[18]

Young people from black and minority ethnic groups will experience worse long-term employment outcomes compared with those from young white groups. The EHRC states: 'In 2015, there were 41,000 16 to 24 year olds from ethnic minorities who were long-term unemployed, a rise of 49% since 2010. This is compared with a fall of 1% in overall long-term youth unemployment and a 2% fall in unemployment among young white people'.[19] The EHRC also suggests that Muslim groups have experienced the worst outcomes in employment compared with all other ethnic groups, with variations between Muslim men and Muslim women. Muslim groups as a whole have experienced the worst unemployment rates and the lowest levels of employment across England, Scotland and Wales.

Senior decision-making roles

I have discussed elsewhere the lack of black and minority ethnic individuals in professorial and senior decision-making roles in higher education (see Chapter Six). However, such a racialised demarcation is not particular to higher education and similar patterns exist across different professions. For example, if you are black or from a minority ethnic group, you are less likely to be employed as a manager, director or in a senior decision-making role (8.8%) than if you are white (10.7%).[20] The EHRC states that this is particularly the case for those from African Caribbean/black backgrounds (5.7%) and mixed ethnicity backgrounds (7.2%). This inequality suggests that '[b]y the end of 2014, ethnic minority representation in Financial Times Stock Exchange (FTSE) 100 boardrooms was 5%. All white teams ran 69% of FTSE 100 companies and 95% of FTSE 100 board directors were white'[21] and there are only two FTSE 100 companies with an ethnic minority person as chair. In the public sector the numbers of black and minority ethnic individuals in senior roles saw an increase from 4% in 1988 to 10% in 2014; worryingly it was only 7% within the senior Civil Service.[22]

In terms of pay, if you are black or from a minority ethnic group you are more likely to be paid less than your white counterparts. Pakistani/Bangladeshi and 'other' ethnic groups received lower pay (an average of less than £10 per hour in 2013) compared with white groups. While Bangladeshi men have the lowest rates of pay, it is black men and their families who have seen the biggest regression in pay and income since 2010.[23]

If you are from a black and Asian background, you are more likely to be in a low-paid job than if you are from a white background. 'The number of Black and Asian workers in low paid jobs increased by 12.7% between 2011 and 2014, compared with a 1.8% increase for white workers ... and both Sikhs and Muslims have the highest pay gap compared with those with no religion, earning around 20% less in 2013'.[24] Higher education qualifications do not make a difference to these inequalities.

Recent research suggests that black workers with degrees earn 23.1% less on average than white workers with degrees. This suggests the differential pay gap is at its widest for those with university degrees.[25] Black workers earn £14.33 per hour compared with £18.62 for white workers. Having 'A' levels does not make any difference to the ethnic differential in earnings. Black workers with 'A' levels earn 14.3% less on average than their white counterparts and black people who leave school with GCSEs are paid 11.4% less than their white peers. 'The pay gap between white workers and all ethnic minority groups, regardless of their educational attainment is 5.6%, and is 12.8% for Black workers'.[26.]

Recent research suggests that parental background and geographical location are significant determinants for labour market outcomes if you are from a black or minority ethnic group rather than if you are a white British graduate: 'Ethnic minority graduates who do not benefit from financial support from their parents earn less and are less likely to be employed compared with white British graduates in the same situation'.[27] Black and minority ethnic women from disadvantaged backgrounds earn less than white women, while black Caribbean, black African and Pakistani graduates from disadvantaged backgrounds earn less than white male British graduates.[28]

Ethnic penalties in the labour market

While there is ample evidence to suggest that there has been an increase in the numbers of people from black and minority ethnic backgrounds entering and being successful in higher education, they are less likely to graduate from prestigious elite Russell Group universities even when they have the same qualifications on entry.[29] Getting a good education may be part of a strategic choice for families to counter discrimination in the labour market,[30] but this does not in itself reduce the ethnic penalties that black and minority ethnic workers experience in the labour market. Rather, those from black and minority ethnic backgrounds are more likely to be in jobs for which they are over-qualified[31] and are less likely to find employment in the first place compared with their white counterparts.[32]

Getting a good job is often dependent on access to social networks and connections which enable links to be made and in turn lead to introductions and job offers. For many black and minority ethnic families, these connections simply do not exist. Many black and minority ethnic parents may not have access to such social networks and contacts[33] and many may lack the skills and access to social capital which provide them with resources to make such connections.[34] Parents from white middle-class backgrounds are more likely to have both the social connections and financial resources to promote their children's best interests, for example by securing and finding unpaid internships that lead to future lucrative employment.[35]

Li's research[36] suggests that even when black and minority ethnic groups have similar levels of educational attainment, this does not result in equal outcomes in the labour market. 'Overall, the evidence suggests that even with similar demo-geographical attributes, higher educational achievement failed to protect ethnic minority men and women against unemployment, especially when the economic situation was bad, such as during the 1980s, 1990s and in the current recession'.[37] The ethnic penalties that black and minority ethnic groups face can take many forms. One clear reason for this is the discrimination and racism they face, not only in gaining access to jobs, but also the racism and discrimination they encounter once employed. 'In spite of their higher qualifications, ethnic minorities, particularly black people and Muslims encounter dual disadvantages, firstly in employment and then, when in work, in gaining career advancement'.[38]

Access to social networks

Access to social networks can also affect gaining access to employment or the means by which employment can be sought. Parents with fewer resources lack access to social networks, creating further inequalities in gaining access to the jobs – and particular types of jobs – in the labour market.[39] Some studies have suggested that individuals from black and minority ethnic backgrounds are more likely than their white counterparts to want to work in their more familiar local area[40] and are more likely to live in poorer areas where they have less access to well-paid jobs.[41]

Geographical location

Zwysen and Longhi argue that geographical location has a significant impact on labour market outcomes, 'The local area can influence labour market outcomes through the local opportunities available as well as through the local network which can help people with their job search. Although these can be personal networks, graduates entering the labour market are likely to rely heavily on their parents' networks'.[42] Their research shows clear evidence of ethnic penalties in the labour market: 'Even after controlling for early employment status black Caribbean woman, black African and Indian men and women and Pakistani women are still less likely to be employed three and a half years after graduation'.[43] The authors also suggest that ethnic gaps in employment and earnings are greater when black and ethnic minority groups lack access to social networks which would enable them to get a job (as discussed above). 'Graduates from a working-class background who come from an area with a small and low educated co-ethnic community earn on average about 5% less than their white British peers six months after graduation'.[44]

Locality and geography play a key role in access to jobs.

> While there is some commonality between groups (particularly at the regional level), the *local* geography of ethnic unemployment is distinct; there is no clear consistency in which places do better and or worse in employment between ethnic groups. The relationship between ethnic group population size and labour market outcomes is complex and variable between ethnic groups.[45]

In their recommendations, Catney and Sabater suggest that the racism and discrimination faced by black and minority ethnic groups in access to and within the labour market must be addressed. 'More interventionist policies are needed to ensure that labour market discrimination is eradicated. This may mean having more effective anti-discrimination legislation to combat prejudice, stereotypes and popular beliefs which emerge from a lack of understanding of cultures other than the majority one'.[46] They also recommend that '[t]he public sector should be at the forefront of recruiting people from ethnic minority groups, particularly those who face systematic disadvantage in the labour market ... at the same time, businesses need to be given support to create more diverse workforces'.[47]

The evidence points to the existence and the persistence of ethnic inequalities in the labour market over time.[48] The inequalities and the persistence of ethnic penalties in the labour market exist *within* and *between* different ethnic groups, with some suffering from a greater labour market penalty than others. The ethnic penalty is further linked to location and geography, with those living in poorer areas suffering the highest penalties.[49] 'Geographical location may affect a person's labour market prospects given poor local employment opportunities. Living in a deprived neighbourhood has been shown to have a negative impact on employment prospects, particularly for people affiliating with an ethnic minority group'.[50] Some researchers have referred to this as a 'spatial mismatch', where individuals may not live in areas where work is readily available, and there is a suggestion that this affects those from black and minority ethnic groups more than those from white backgrounds.[51] 'According to the spatial mismatch hypothesis, there are fewer jobs per worker in areas with higher concentrations of immigrant and UK-born ethnic minority groups than in predominantly white areas'.[52]

Ethnic inequalities have persisted over time[53] with black Caribbean, black African and Pakistani/Bangladeshi men being the most disadvantaged.[54] Hudson and Radu[55] suggest that these inequalities continue when black and minority ethnic groups are in work in which they are less likely to gain promotion to senior roles. Recently there is evidence to suggest an increase in self-employment related to some minority ethnic groups, who use this as a route to escape the disadvantages they face in the labour market – such as racism and discrimination.[56] While there have been some winners and losers over time in relation to gains and losses in the labour market, the overall picture is clear. 'The overwhelming picture is one of continuing ethnic minority disadvantage compared with the white British majority group. In terms of unemployment, there is a clear ethnic minority penalty in the labour market, which is persistent over time'.[57] Catney and Sabater[58] suggest that if black and minority ethnic groups are over-represented in some occupations, this will lead to a possible segregation and stereotyping of certain jobs, resulting in processes of discrimination for entry into specific sectors of the labour market.

Analysis of disparities in the labour market suggest that black and minority ethnic groups are not only over-represented in low-skilled occupations, they are under-represented in higher-skilled, high-paying managerial positions, which results in wage inequality and differentials between white and minority ethnic groups whereby minority ethnic groups are disadvantaged.[59]

Inequalities over time?

Occupational segregation is the result of direct and indirect discrimination for entry into specific jobs in which black and minority ethnic groups continue to be disadvantaged. The labour market is a structure in which white privilege continues to dominate. I have argued that while black and minority ethnic groups are increasingly entering higher education', this does not translate into access to and success in the labour market. Many occupations retain their elite status by maintaining and reinforcing their whiteness and white privilege. The most elite, highly paid professions remain white, and black and minority ethnic groups are less likely to hold positions in which they are involved in decision-making roles. For example, black and minority ethnic groups are under-represented in national and local political positions; out of 3,238 judges only 159 are from a black or minority ethnic background (5.9%); black and minority ethnic police officers make up 5.5% of all officers in England and Wales and 11 police forces in England and Wales have no black or minority ethnic police officers above the inspector grade; and as of May 2016 there were no black or minority ethnic chief constables.[60] Many occupations continue to perpetuate whiteness and white privilege whereby being a member of a black or minority ethnic group remains a disadvantage.

Catney and Sabater[61] suggest direct links between poverty and labour market participation. If you are from an ethnic minority and you grew up in a deprived area, you are less likely to attend an elite university and are unlikely to make the connections necessary to achieve a high-status public role in later life.

There is evidence of discrimination based on ethnicity and race which takes place at different points in the labour market – both at the point of entry and during employment.[62] Labour market participation is also affected in times of recession, hitting those from black and minority ethnic communities the hardest. Faced with already existing discrimination in the labour market because of their race and ethnicity, this is further exacerbated when greater numbers of individuals compete for a small number of jobs. This is particularly the case for those from younger age groups. 'Since ethnic minority groups tend to have youthful age structures, it is not unreasonable to expect they have been particularly badly affected by the recession'.[63] Furthermore, Catney and Sabater[64] suggest that this situation may be deteriorating in the public sector, where those from black and minority ethnic groups are over-represented.

Exploring economic activity over time (2001 to 2011) longitudinal research suggests that there are differences between ethnic groups in terms of employment, unemployment and self-employment. There is evidence to suggest that there is a clear 'ethnic penalty' in employment rates, for example '[i]n 2001, unemployment rates were highest for Bangladeshi (18%), African, Mixed white Caribbean and Pakistani groups (16% each)'.[65] One of the ways in which these differences and the 'ethnic penalty' can be explained is by examining the differentials in educational qualifications between different ethnic groups. However, as I have argued elsewhere, those from black and minority ethnic backgrounds are entering higher education in increasing numbers, but they are less likely to leave university with a 2:1 or a first-class degree. And when they have similar qualifications to their white counterparts, they are more likely to be unemployed six months after graduation and earn less.

The statistical evidence suggests that even when education is controlled for, ethnic penalties still exist for black and minority ethnic groups.[66] In terms of representation, some black and minority ethnic groups are under-represented in certain jobs and over-represented in others. 'The systematic economic marginalisation of ethnic minority groups into specific labour markets or niches (labour market segmentation) is an important aspect which adds a further dimension to ethnic inequalities'.[67] Furthermore, there is evidence to suggest that '… ethnic minorities tend to be trapped in lower labour market segments, and that gender and class affects overlap'.[68]

Racism?

The TUC has outlined the harsh realities faced by black and minority ethnic workers in the labour market.

> The harsh reality is that, even now, BME people, regardless of their qualifications and experience, are far more likely to be unemployed and lower paid than white people. Whether they have PhDs or GCSEs, BME workers have a much tougher time in the job market. Not only is this wrong, but it is a huge waste of talent. Companies that only recruit from a narrow base are missing out on the wide range of experiences on offer from Britain's many different communities.[69]

The TUC has asked the government to tackle this issue of inequality, particularly in relation to addressing and developing a race equality strategy with clear objectives and outcomes for equality of opportunity for black and minority ethnic groups in the labour market. They have also suggested greater transparency in career progression and for employers to introduce a process of anonymised applications across the public sector. There is also a need for employers to include ethnicity as a variable in their annual reports in order that transparency and career progression of black and minority ethnic staff can be measured and addressed; particularly to monitor and review their own recruitment processes for discrimination and bias.

A recent report which explored the barriers to progression for black and minority ethnic people found that the lack of black role models in the Civil Service was demoralising and harmful for those who wanted to progress in the Civil Service. The research also found that respondents felt that there was an 'old boys club' and the performance management process was biased and unhelpful. 'Unconscious bias and discrimination persists which can block the progress of talented BME staff and means there is not always equal access to promotion, projects, senior leaders and secondments. All of this limits the aspirations and success of BME staff'.[70]

The Department for Work and Pensions (DWP) in their data analysis of black and minority ethnic staff in the labour market found huge differentials in labour market activity between different ethnic groups, for example '[u]nemployment varies from 14% for the black group to 6.4% for the Indian group'.[71] There are also variations by sector: '... ethnic minority groups are more likely to be employed in sectors relating to accommodation and food services; wholesale and retail trade; transportation and storage and human health and social work activities. They are less likely to be employed in the manufacturing, construction and education sectors'.[72]

Earnings

A recent report published by the TUC found that inequalities continue to exist in the labour market even when black workers have the same qualifications as their white counterparts. For example, black workers with degrees earn 23.1% less on average than white workers with degrees. The TUC report found that a black worker with a degree will earn £14.33 an hour (on average) compared with a white graduate who will earn £18.63 an hour – which is £4.33 more. The pay gap between white and black workers is greatest at degree level. 'Black workers with "A" levels earn 14.3% less on average than their white counterparts. And black people who leave school with GCSEs typically get paid 11.4% less than their white peers. The gap between all black, Asian and minority ethnic (BAME) workers with degrees and white graduates is 10.3% – the equivalent of £1.93 per hour'.[73]

Table 8.2: Employees: gross hourly pay

	White workers	All BAME workers		Black workers	
	Pay	Pay	Pay gap	Pay	Pay gap
All workers	£13.45	£12.70	5.6%	£11.73	12.8%
Degree	£18.63	£16.70	10.3%	£14.33	23.1%
A-levels	£11.53	£9.55	17.1%	£9.88	14.3%
GCSE (A* - C equivalent)	£10.33	£8.93	13.6%	£9.15	11.4%
No qualifications	£8.90	£8.25	7.3%	£9.00	-1.1%
Other qualifications	£9.48	£8.88	6.3%	£9.25	2.4%

Source: Trade Unions Congress (2016).

The following section explores two case studies of UK students who are in the final year of their undergraduate degrees, both of whom are expecting to make successful transitions into the labour market.

JONATHAN

Jonathan describes himself as a black British male. He has one sister who is training to be a vet and he is in his final year of studying Politics at a Russell Group university in a large city. He is on track to get a 2:1 degree and wants to go straight into the labour market and work in journalism. Jonathan was sceptical of his chances of getting a job. While he knew that he would have to ensure he got a 2:1 at the end, which would help him to get a job, he felt it was his ethnicity that would be the determining factor for employment.

'I know that I have to get a good degree and I know that I can have some control over that – to an extent – I can work hard and make sure that I aim for a 2:1 and then get it. Hopefully that should happen because I have been getting good marks, so it should just carry on. The things that worry me about getting a job are the amount of competition there is out there at the moment. You're competing with all kinds of people who have more qualifications and more experience, so that is one thing. But that competition will be there no matter what. For me it is the things you can't control like the discrimination I will face when going for a job.'

Jonathan did not feel that such overt discrimination existed in higher education, he felt that discrimination in the labour market was far more overt and based on how employers wanted their own organisations to be portrayed and the image they wanted to reinforce.

'I worry more about getting an interview and not being able to get a job because I am a black male. I know it is harder if you are black anyway, but being a male there are certain stereotypes people have of you and they might not want a black male to work for them. I know that might sound a bit negative but I have heard of these stories when black people turn up for jobs and you don't get it and you know it's because they just don't want a black person to represent their organisation.'

Jonathan also felt that the situation had deteriorated in the current economic and political climate.

'I think there are lots of reasons for me to feel we are going back to what it was like for my parents – that open way of being racist – that has come back and there is a certain mood now, that maybe wasn't there before, that says you are not wanted because of your race. That kind of thing worries me a lot and I wonder if I am going to leave university with a degree and then be unemployed. That would be very depressing and very worrying.'

Jonathan felt that much of this 'mood' was related to political events such as Brexit and the recent election of Donald J Trump as 45th President of the United States, as well as the scarcity of jobs.

'These are sad, difficult times. If you think about all the political turmoil and terrorism, I think people are scared that things might go wrong for them so that means they will keep employing people who are like them – they are white – and the media and other events reinforce that ideal – to keep the system as it is and safe. At the same time, there is more competition for jobs because more people are going for jobs so employers can become more selective and think well, I don't want that black person working for me, there are plenty of white people that I can employ in my company.'

Jonathan was not yet considering postgraduate study because he could not afford to pay the fees and preferred to work.

'I don't want to do a Masters, I want to get a job. But I have to see how that goes, but if I don't get a job I can't carry on studying because it's far too expensive for me. I would like to think that I am not going to be discriminated against because I am a black male and that I will be judged based on my degree – but I think I may be naive in thinking that way.'

Jonathan spoke about the different types of employment that he felt were discriminatory.

'I guess it depends on the type of employment, if you go into a profession that is mainly white then you will get discriminated against – but if you go into something where there are lots of black people – it works differently.'

Asked about which professions Jonathan was referring to, he responded:

'Like in my university all the people who work in the canteen are black women and most of the cleaners are black, and in my department there are no black lecturers.'

NEEMA

While Jonathan said it was his ethnicity and gender that would affect whether he would get a job, Neema, on the other hand, felt that employers would discriminate against her because of her religion and ethnicity. Neema described herself as a British Muslim; she wore a headscarf and was proud to be a Muslim but was worried about leaving university to enter the labour market.

'In some ways you are safe here – in the university – people are nice and if they are racist then they don't show it to your face – but they are nice. I am worried when I leave here and have to look for a job. I have seen how the way people treat Muslims has changed since Brexit and Donald Trump who wants to ban Muslims. This is happening all over the world now. We are seen as being the ones to blame for terrorism when it has nothing to do with us.'

Neema felt that she would be discriminated against for wearing a headscarf and being a Muslim.

'I think even though I know I am going to get a good degree, it is not how I am going to be judged. It will be based on what I am wearing and what I look like. I think there is already racism out there and when you are wearing a scarf it just magnifies it all so much, because it is visible and you can see it. It is saying this is me and this is what I believe in and many places don't want that representation and so just won't give you a job based on that. They are also afraid because they might think that if they have a Muslim woman working for them, it could affect how people see them and the company.'

Neema, like Jonathan also felt that the situation had deteriorated since recent political and social events.

'There have been lots of people who have said to me that they have people shouting at them after the EU vote and that is very upsetting. I think we Muslims have become the scapegoat for things that are happening and this blame is going on all over the world, not just here in the UK.'

Conclusions

The increase in racist incidents post Brexit has further marginalised black and minority ethnic communities. This contributes to the prevailing inequalities experienced by black and minority ethnic groups in the labour market. Even when black and minority ethnic groups have similar qualifications to their white counterparts, they still earn less, are in lower-skilled occupations and are more likely to be unemployed.

White privilege in the labour market is an example of covert and overt processes which work to keep black and minority ethnic groups excluded from senior decision-making roles and positions of power. Whiteness operates to exclude black and minority ethnic groups from certain professions. Consequently, black and minority groups (even when they are highly qualified) suffer an ethnic penalty in the labour market.

As a result, sections of the labour market are reserved for whites only – positions where whiteness is used to reinforce power and status. Despite the emphasis on diversity and equality of opportunity, vast ethnic inequalities continue to persist in the labour market. The pressure on organisations to abide by equality legislation is just that – all public bodies have a duty to abide by such legislation. But this does not demonstrate that they value diversity or indeed fight for equality of opportunity. Instead, such legislation perpetuates the myth that inclusion is a reality. Organisations value whiteness and the privilege that white identity brings, and white groups work to protect their own position of dominance and advantage – at all costs.

NINE

Wealth, poverty and inequality

This chapter will explore how race affects wealth, poverty and inequality. An increasing number of black and minority ethnic groups continue to live in low-income households, which affects their future opportunities including access to higher education and the labour market. This chapter will argue that poverty and inequality is related to processes of racism, which has a significant impact on the future life choices and life chances of black and minority ethnic young people, both in the UK and the US.

Who is poor?

The previous chapter explored the vast inequalities that continue to exist for black and minority people in the labour market. There is evidence to suggest that these inequalities have a direct impact on poverty levels for these groups. Catney and Sabater suggest that '[p]overty does not affect all ethnic groups equally, with ethnic minority groups more likely to experience poverty than the majority white group'.[1] There is also evidence to suggest that there are differences in economic inequality and the effect this has on poverty levels *within* and *between* different black and minority ethnic groups (for example in terms of gender and ethnicity).[2] As a result, the inequalities that black and minority ethnic groups experience in the labour market have a direct impact on the poverty they experience – both for individuals and households.[3] Furthermore, geographical location also has a significant impact on whether individuals experience poverty and the *types* and *extent* of poverty they will experience.[4]

Geographical location has a significant impact on being able to find work and the availability of work, which has a knock-on effect on poverty levels. Those who are looking for work but do not live in areas where work is available experience a 'spatial mismatch' between job supply and job demand – and this will affect people from different ethnic minority groups in different ways. Catney and Sabater suggest that '[a]ccording to the spatial mismatch hypothesis, there are fewer jobs per worker in areas with higher concentrations of immigrant and UK born ethnic minority groups than in predominantly white areas'.[5] Menash[6] has argued that black and minority ethnic workers are more likely than other groups to want to live near their place of work.[7] This has a knock-on effect on those who live in poverty as they are less likely to be able to afford to move to areas where there are higher levels of employment available to them.

The longer-term impact of such 'spatial mismatches' suggests that the links between poverty, ethnicity and location may result in the segregation of different communities.[8] This may include the concentration of certain black and minority ethnic groups in specific areas, which will further impact on the experiences of poverty. In order to address these inequalities it is important to examine how black and minority ethnic groups perform in the labour market and the implications this has for tackling inequality both in the labour market and in society more generally.[9] In areas where there are fewer jobs, this may result in greater competition for jobs, with some groups being more disadvantaged than others. Furthermore, this may cause high rates of unemployment or lead to the availability of part-time work, when workers are in fact seeking full-time employment. Such inequalities may result in unequal access to certain types of jobs, resulting in some groups being overqualified for available employment.

The recession has also had an impact on poverty levels; average wages have not increased in line with inflation and consequently there has been a decline in overall living standards. But this is not experienced uniformly across the population as a whole. Young graduates were badly hit by the recession even though they had degree-level qualifications.[10] The evidence suggests that it was those from black and minority ethnic groups who were worst hit as such groups tend to have younger age structures.[11]

Different explanations for poverty

Housing

The Equality and Human Rights Commission (EHRC)[12] in their recent report point out that there are different ways of understanding poverty and how it impacts on the lives of individuals and their families. If you are from a black or minority ethnic background you are more likely to live in substandard housing than if you are white. Substandard housing is housing that does not meet the requirements for health and safety and may pose a risk to the health, safety and physical well-being of its occupants.

The EHRC found that in 2011/12 in England, 27.9% of black people and 26.3% of Pakistani/Bangladeshi people lived in substandard housing compared with 20.5% of those from white backgrounds. Furthermore, children living in families from Pakistani/Bangladeshi backgrounds (28.6%) and black backgrounds (24.2%) were more likely to be living in substandard housing than those from white backgrounds (18.6%). There is clear evidence that such living conditions can impact on the health, well-being and educational progress of young children.[13]

Black and minority ethnic groups are also more likely to be living in overcrowded housing than white groups; 21.7% Pakistani/Bangladeshi, 15.7% of black groups and 13.4% of Indian groups were living in overcrowded housing compared with 3.4% of white households (2012/13). Children from all of these groups were also more likely to live in overcrowded housing than children from white groups.[14]

Material deprivation

Black and minority ethnic groups had a higher child poverty rate in 2012/13 than white groups. While there are differences within the black and minority ethnic category, the evidence suggests that black and minority ethnic groups are more likely to

145

be in poverty than the white group. So, for example, Pakistani/ Bangladeshi, African Caribbean/black and other groups have a higher child poverty rate compared with white groups.[15]

Pakistani/Bangladeshi, African/Caribbean/black and 'other' groups who are of working age have a higher mean deprivation score compared with the white groups. Deprivation is defined as lack of income and lack of adequate resources required for a suitable standard of living. Consequently, individuals from black and minority ethnic groups (35.7%) were more likely to be living in poverty than white groups (17.2%) in 2012/13.[16]

The EHRC data uses the concept of relative poverty, which is the percentage of people living in households below 60% of the median income.[17] Children who lived in households headed by those from a black or minority ethnic background (41.9%) were more likely to be living in poverty than those headed by a white individual (24.5%). Children from Pakistani/Bangladeshi, black or other backgrounds were more likely to have higher poverty rates compared with other groups.[18] The EHRC states:

> More recent data shows significant differences in the proportion of people in poverty by ethnicity – poverty is up to twice as likely among ethnic minorities as it is for white people. The poverty rate has been consistently lowest among white people. In 2014/15, it was 19%. The proportion of black or black British people in poverty has increased by four percentage points and by 10 percentage points for those from other backgrounds since 2002/03.[19]

A recent report published by the Runnymede Trust[20] found that individuals from black and minority ethnic groups would suffer greater negative impacts as a result of the changes of the 2015 budget compared with those from white groups, suggesting that a total of 1.25 million black and minority ethnic households would be worse off. Figure 9.1 shows the numbers of people living in poverty, indicating that those from black and minority ethnic backgrounds are more likely to be living in poverty compared with white groups.[21]

Figure 9.1: Proportion of people in poverty by ethnicity

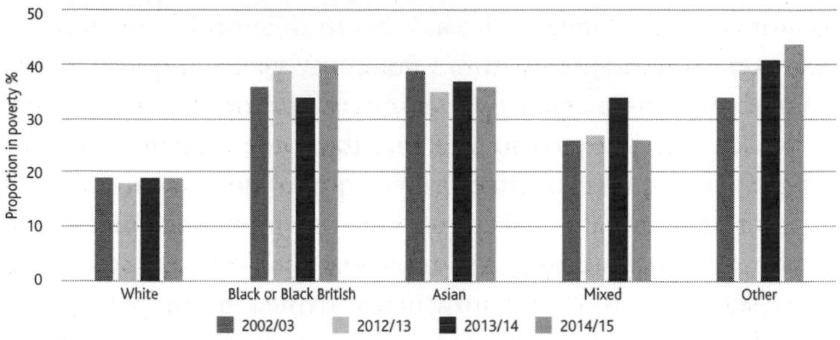

Source: Households Below Average Income (HBAI), 2016.

A recent report examining the impact of the recession and austerity measures, (2004/5–2007/8 and 2009/10–2012/13) found significant differences by ethnic group.[22] The report found that those from Pakistani and Bangladeshi backgrounds were more likely to experience persistent poverty and those from black African and black Caribbean groups had the highest rates of persistent poverty and found it much harder to escape from poverty. In comparison, white groups had persistent lower rates of poverty and higher rates of never being poor. Those living in poverty who are consistently poor are more likely to live in social housing, tend to be younger, are less likely to have a degree and are more likely to be unemployed compared with those who are not living in poverty or those who are persistently poor.[23]

Neighbourhoods

I have discussed elsewhere in this book how black and minority ethnic groups are more likely to be unemployed than white groups. I have argued that one reason for this is the result of overt and covert discrimination by which the processes of white privilege are perpetuated and reinforced. Disadvantages in the labour market are likely to be related to disadvantages linked to poverty (such as deprivation, housing and health). Furthermore, if individuals from black and minority ethnic groups are living in deprived areas, this may further restrict their opportunities for highly skilled, well-paid employment and mobility in the labour market. Jivraj and Khan refer to this as a 'double disadvantage'. 'This refers to the combined effect of individual and neighbourhood disadvantage, for example being unemployed in an area of high unemployment'.[24]

There is evidence to suggest that black and minority ethnic groups are more likely than white groups to live in deprived neighbourhoods. Pakistani and Bangladeshi groups (more than one in three) and black, African and Caribbean groups (more than one in five) were more likely to live in deprived areas compared with fewer than one in 12 for white British groups.[25]

Health

Health and well-being can have a significant impact on future life chances in relation to education and employment[26] and there are inequalities in who suffers from ill-health and who has access to good healthcare. If you are black or from a minority ethnic background you are more likely to suffer from health problems and are less likely to have access to good health care than if you are white.[27]

Mental health

The recent evidence compiled by the EHRC found that black people were more likely than other groups to suffer from poor mental health; they were more likely to have higher rates of being admitted to hospital, have longer hospital stays and be more likely to be readmitted into hospital than other groups. The EHRC states that '[i]n 2014, the probability of Black African women being detained under the Mental Health Act 1983 in England and Wales was more than seven times higher than for white British women'.[28] Gypsies and Travellers also had poor access to health care; particularly registering for a GP and having access to primary care.

If you are from a Pakistani/Bangladeshi or black African/Caribbean background you are more likely to be at risk of poor mental health compared with the white majority group. If you are a woman from a Pakistani/Bangladeshi background you are more likely to be at risk from poor mental health (28.2%) than if you are a white woman (17.4%).[29] A recent study[30] found that during the period 2014/15 black groups had spent more time in hospital compared with any other ethnic group. The same study also found that black groups were more likely to be admitted to hospital for psychiatric problems than individuals from other ethnic groups.

Physical health

There are differences in the physical health of individuals by ethnic group. Black Caribbean people were more likely than other minority ethnic groups to report health that was 'not good'. Furthermore, individuals from black and minority ethnic backgrounds are more likely to have lower access to palliative and end-of-life care services compared with white British people. These findings are based on lack of referrals and experiences based on accessing care.[31] There is also evidence to suggest that many people from black and minority ethnic backgrounds feel there is a lack of information available in different languages and relevant information on different family and religious values. Furthermore, where people die may be associated with ethnicity: 'On the whole, ethnic minorities are more likely to die in hospital and less likely to die at home or in a hospice than white people, but there are important differences between ethnicities'.[32]

Poverty in the US

In the US, there is recent evidence to suggest that black Americans are more likely than white Americans to be living in poverty. A total of 27% of all African American men, women and children live below the poverty line compared with 11% of all Americans.[33] Black children are also more likely to live in poverty (38%) compared with 22% of all children in the US. Furthermore, the poverty rate for black working-age women is 26% compared with 21% for black working-age men.[34]

There are differences between family types, with 8% of black married families living in poverty compared with 37% of single female families. Black female single-parent families have the highest poverty rates at 46%.[35]

According to recent figures released by the US Census Bureau in 2014, a total of 14.8% of people lived in poverty. Between 1993 and 2000, the poverty rate saw a fall year on year but since 2000 there has been a slow increase in the number of people living in poverty.[36] There are vast differences in poverty across different ethnic groups. For example, if you are black or Hispanic you are more likely than other groups to live in poverty. In 2014, a total of 26.2% of black people and 23.6% of Hispanics were living in poverty compared with 10.1% of non–Hispanic whites and 12% of Asians.[37] Women from black or Hispanic single-parent backgrounds were more likely to be living in poverty than any other ethnic group. A total of 30.6% of single female households in 2014 were living in poverty compared with 15.7% of single male households and 6.2% of married-couple households.

In the US, it is children who represent the majority of individuals who live in poverty. While children make up 23.1% of the total population, they make up 33.3% of those living in poverty. Data from 2014 suggests that 15.5 million children (21.1%) were living in poverty. Children who are black, American Indian or Hispanic are more likely to be living in poverty than white children.[38]

Parental education also has an effect on whether children are more or less likely to live in poverty. If parents have high levels of education their children are less likely to live in poverty. A total of 12% of children who come from a family where one parent has a college education live in poverty compared with 55% in families where parents have less than a high school qualification. Parental employment also has an effect on whether children live in poverty. If parents are employed all year round then children are less likely to live in poverty compared with those who are employed intermittently or work part time. For example, a total of 74% of children who have no parent who works full time live in poverty.[39]

Children who live with married parents are less likely to be poor or in low-income families than those who live in single-parent families; 41% of children living in single-parent families live in poverty. There is also evidence to suggest that stable living arrangements have a significant impact on health and well-being.[40] Jiang et al state: 'Children living in low-income families are nearly twice as likely as other children to have moved in the past year and nearly three times as likely to live in families who rent, rather than own their own homes'.[41] Children who live in poverty as also less likely to be covered by health insurance.[42]

Figure 9.2: Percentage of children in low income/poverty by ethnicity

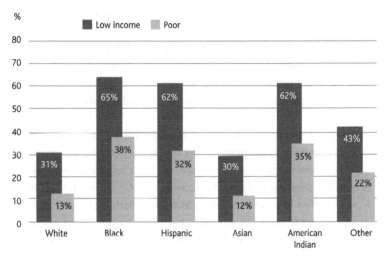

Source: US National Centre for Children in Poverty (http://www.nccp.org/publications/pub_1145.html).

Long term effects of poverty: segregation and exclusion

A recent report published by the Century Foundation suggests that recent events in the US that have resulted in civil unrest – such as the killing of black men by white police officers – are the result of long-term poverty and inequality in the US. The report's author, Paul Jargowsky, suggests:

> [s]omething important however, is being left out of this conversation; namely that we are witnessing a nationwide return of concentrated poverty that is racial in nature and that this expansion and continued existence of high poverty ghettos and barrios is no

accident. These neighbourhoods are not the value free outcome of the impartial workings of the housing market. Rather, in large measure, they are the inevitable and predictable consequences of deliberate policy choices.[43]

Jargowsy suggests that policy choices were deliberately made to increase segregation and these policy choices disadvantage some groups (blacks and Hispanics) and advantage others (whites). Jargowsy argues that there has been an increase in the number of high-poverty neighbourhoods; the number of people living in high-poverty neighbourhoods (such as slums, ghettos and barrios) has more than doubled in the last decade. If you are black or Hispanic you are more likely to live in these areas. Furthermore, there has been an increase in black poverty in metropolitan areas in the US and it is children who are more likely than adults to live in high poverty areas.[44] Jargowsy argues that policies were designed to keep areas selective, in this sense neighbourhoods were able to maintain their exclusivity by using policy making to enforce discrimination. 'The population movements were also highly selective. Through exclusionary zoning and outright housing market discrimination, the upper middle class and affluent could move to the suburbs and the poor were left behind. Public and assisted housing units were often constructed in ways that reinforced existing spatial disparities'.[45]

As a result of gentrification there is a movement of the poor out of cities and into deprived and decaying 'inner-ring suburbs'. Policies are designed to keep certain neighbourhoods selective and this process is

> legally enforced through zoning and underwritten by the mortgage interest deduction and all the subsidies that go into building roads, sewers and schools for the new suburbs and institutional arrangements that are too often taken for granted. Our governance and development practices ensure that significant segments of our population live in neighbourhoods where there is no water, where there are under

performing schools and where there is little access
to opportunity.[46]

And these richer areas are white and the poorer areas are
populated by black and minority ethnic groups such as Hispanics.
There is also recent evidence to suggest that greater income
inequality is linked to more deaths of black African Americans.[47]

A recent study conducted by researchers at the University
of California, Berkeley found that income inequality may be
a proxy for racial segregation, especially for black people. The
report's author, Nuru-Jeter, suggests that '[r]acial segregation
and concentrated poverty can't be completely disentangled from
income inequality. In our study, racial segregation completely
explained the effect of income inequality on mortality among
blacks'.[48]

Place matters and being black suggests that where you live
will have a significant impact on your life chances. 'The idea is
that the sense of being left behind, of not making it, of living in
an area where there is more crime, more pollution, fewer jobs,
lower-quality schools, less access to parks and green space, all
come with stressors that impact health'.[49] Recent research carried
out by the Pew Research Center found that while there has been
an overall decline in the number of children living in poverty, this
is not the case for black children. The number of black children
living in poverty has changed little and they are the group most
likely to be living in poverty. The Pew Research Center found
that black and Hispanic children are over-represented in the
figures on poverty. In contrast, children from white and Asian
populations make up roughly equal shares of the child population
and those living in poverty.[50]

Conclusions

I have discussed in previous chapters the disadvantaged positions
that those from black and minority ethnic backgrounds find
themselves in, at all levels of society. There is evidence to suggest
that black and minority ethnic groups are less likely to have
the same opportunities as white groups in their access to well-
funded schools and elite universities. They are less likely to leave

university with a 2:1 or first-class degree compared with white students and when they enter the labour market they are further disadvantaged. These inequalities together have a cumulative effect on why some black and minority ethnic groups both in the UK and the US end up living in poverty or in low-income households.

In the US, black African American people are more likely to attend underfunded public schools, live in socially deprived areas, and be discriminated against in the criminal justice system compared with white groups, which has knock-on effects on future life chances available to them.[51]

Inequalities in access to decent schools and housing create inequalities between different ethnic groups based on race. The prevalence and predominance of whiteness and white privilege work to perpetuate the inferior and powerless position of black and minority ethnic groups – *to keep them in their place*. Whiteness works to maintain and protect white privilege – at all costs – consequently systems and structures are designed to do this. An example of this is the segregation of different ethnic groups living in specific neighbourhoods (both in the UK and the US). The best schools are in areas which are predominantly white and middle class where many black and minority ethnic people cannot afford to live. Tax laws and policies are designed to keep the poor (black and minority ethnic groups) out of wealthier areas. Consequently, their children are unable to attend the best well-funded schools, which has knock-on effects for future life chances such as access to good universities and social mobility in the labour market. A system of privilege is maintained so that whiteness and white privilege are reinforced and continue to be self-perpetuated.

TEN

Conclusions: race, social justice and equality

In this chapter, I bring together previous discussions and suggest ways forward to engage with a social justice and inclusive agenda for change in which the voices and lives of black and minority groups can be represented. I specifically focus on how change can be implemented in the UK education system where white privilege should be addressed and challenged. I argue that in a neoliberal context, policy making has contributed to maintaining the *status quo* in which a post-racial society remains a myth, and covert and overt forms of racism and exclusion continue to operate at all levels in society; in short, white identities are privileged and remain protected at all times.

In this book I have focussed on specific areas that demonstrate how whiteness and white privilege operates. Each of the chapters outlines the position of black and minority ethnic groups and examines evidence to show how they remain disadvantaged in societies where whiteness and white privilege predominate. In Chapter Two I explored how those from black and minority ethnic groups remain disadvantaged in different areas of life, both in the UK and the US. Despite differences between these two countries, whiteness operates as a form of privilege and in current discourse has been used as a rhetoric to reinforce the identity of whiteness as superior. Examples include the recent vote by the British people to leave the EU, fuelled by a reinforcement of 'British' identity and the threat of an invasion of immigrants on British shores. The leave result was followed by a significant rise in the numbers of racist and hate crimes being reported to the police and other anti-racism organisations. Brexit was an 'us versus them' battle in which white privilege was used to separate those who belonged and those who did not, and racism was used as a vehicle to promote this.

In the US, there has been an increase in the numbers of black men being shot by police officers and the numbers continue to rise. The fragility of race relations has further been reinforced by the recent election of Donald J. Trump as the 45th president of the United States. Trump used and continues to use his privilege, wealth and white identity to attack minority groups. In Trump's rhetoric Mexicans are rapists and all Muslims potential terrorists, and because of this he will build a wall to stop Mexicans entering the US and place travel bans on Muslims. Trump's racist and xenophobic comments sparked protest and violence during his presidential campaign. Just as the Brexiteers said 'we want our country back', Donald J. Trump's mantra is to 'make America great again'. Trump has used his whiteness as a form of privilege, which enables him to use racism as a vehicle to promote his cause.

In Chapter Three I argued that it is a particular kind of whiteness that is privileged and protected. I suggest that there are *acceptable* and *non-acceptable* forms of whiteness. Acceptable forms of whiteness are based on the intersections of class, whiteness and white privilege. Non-acceptable forms of whiteness are based on possessing a whiteness which is undesirable and not associated with the privileges whiteness entails. Gypsies and Travellers possess undesirable forms of whiteness. I argue that Gypsies and Travellers experience vast disadvantages in society – in relation to their experiences in the education system, access to housing, poor health and poverty. Furthermore, media images of Gypsies and Travellers continue to demonise and pathologises them as dirty, thieving and at the same time overtly flamboyant and extravagant. In schools, for example, Gypsy and Traveller groups perform poorly in all levels of education and furthermore they continue to experience racism, marginalisation and exclusion in the school space. As groups who sit on the margins of society, whose needs are not considered worthy to be addressed, Gypsies and Travellers constitute a new underclass, forgotten and ignored. The white identity of Gypsy and Traveller groups is not an acceptable privileged form of whiteness – quite the opposite – it is one that is identified by dirt, poverty and unacceptable forms of behaviour. Consequently, the racism that is fuelled by the media against Gypsy and Traveller groups is legitimised and rarely challenged. It is a racism that is acceptable towards an unacceptable form of whiteness.

In Chapter Four, I explored the importance of intersectionality in examining how experiences based on class, gender and race impact in different ways for different groups. I suggested that white identity predominates, but this white identity is also related to class identity. White middle-class identity is privileged above all others, and this takes place in significant ways in higher education. I explore how policy making in higher education has worked to strengthen and advantage the position of white middle-class women at the expense of black and minority ethnic and working-class women. Within higher education institutions, black and minority ethnic academics remain marginalised at all levels; they are less likely to be professors and occupy senior decision-making roles. The white space of the academy continues to perpetuate and reinforce white middle-class privilege. Higher education institutions work to reinforce their own position by perpetuating and protecting their own image as white spaces.

In Chapter Five, I explored specifically the schooling experiences of black and minority ethnic groups and argued that children's experience of schooling is affected by their race and in turn their class. I suggested that educational disadvantage experienced at an early age for black and minority ethnic groups can have a significant impact on future life chances and that within a neoliberal context, policy making in education has failed to address the problems and issues faced by black and minority ethnic groups. Recent changes in policy making and government priorities have pushed race into insignificance. Rather, race is only prioritised in relation to negative stereotypes of black and minority ethnic groups – for example the scrapping of the legal requirement on schools to report racism and the recent introduction of the Prevent strategy. The lack of importance of race within an inclusive policy agenda is further demonstrated in how teachers understand and deal with racism in schools. Teachers report receiving little training on this issue, hence are less likely to know how to deal with racism and racist incidents.

In Chapter Six I focussed specifically on higher education and examined how higher education continues to be dominated by a white elite. Figures suggest that black and minority academics are less likely to be in professorial or senior decision-making roles. There is also recent evidence to suggest that black and minority ethnic academics are more likely to experience racism and exclusion which is subtle, covert and nuanced. I argued that universities want to maintain their position of dominance and do so by perpetuating their whiteness and white dominance. This takes place not only through the lack of representation of black and minority ethnic academics in senior roles, but also through the teaching of a Eurocentric curriculum and specific approaches to equality and diversity. While there has been an increase in the numbers of black and minority ethnic students attending universities, they are less likely to attend elite Russell Group universities and are less likely than white students to leave with a 2:1 or a first-class degree. Universities, by perpetuating their privilege of whiteness, reinforce their identities as being reserved for the privileged few.

In Chapter Seven I focussed on how processes of racism and bullying operate in schools and higher education. There is evidence to suggest that there has been an increase in the numbers of children who report racist bullying. Much of this reporting is related to racism and Islamophobia. Furthermore, many of these incidents have been serious enough to warrant a fixed or permanent exclusion. There is also evidence to suggest high numbers of incidents of reporting racism and bullying in higher education institutions. This takes different forms and recent evidence suggests that black and minority ethnic people are less likely to be put forward for promotion and many report experiencing bullying and racism from managers and colleagues. When complaints about bullying are made either by parents about their children's school experiences or by academics working in higher education institutions, white privilege operates to protect white identities. When complaints about racism are made these are either dismissed as a 'clash of personalities' or parents being 'over protective'. Within a neoliberal context, policy making is used to further reinforce white privilege so that whiteness remains unchallenged.

In Chapter Eight I focussed on racial inequalities in the labour market. I suggested that through racist and exclusionary processes, black and minority ethnic groups are less likely to occupy positions of power in the labour market. While black and minority ethnic young people are entering higher education in significant numbers, this is not reflected in positive experiences in the labour market. When black and minority ethnic people have the same or similar qualifications as their white counterparts, they earn less, are in lower-skilled occupations and more likely to be unemployed. White privilege operates in the labour market to keep black and minority ethnic groups out of certain professions which maintain their own status of whiteness and white privilege. Despite an emphasis on equality and diversity and the existence of policy making in which organisations have to comply with equality legislation, vast inequalities continue to persist in the labour market.

In Chapter Nine, I examined how race affects access to wealth, poverty and inequality. If you are black or from a minority ethnic group you are more likely to live in a low-income household, which has a significant impact on future life chances such as access to higher education and making successful transitions into the labour market. Inequalities in the labour market can have a direct impact on poverty levels for those from black and minority ethnic groups. A system of privilege is maintained and reinforced which works to perpetuate and self-perpetuate whiteness in access to jobs, housing, income and wealth. These inequalities have a cumulative effect on the lives of black and minority ethnic groups. Consequently, those from black and minority ethnic groups who are trapped in cycles of poverty are less likely to be able to move out of the poverty cycle.

How can we move forward in a society that continues to reinforce inequality based on skin colour? The evidence of persistent inequality driven by white privilege suggests significant changes are needed in order to address and challenge racial inequalities. While racism may never be eradicated this does not mean we cannot actively challenge white groups who occupy positions of power and use white privilege as a means of protecting their position and their power. One setting where radical changes are both urgently needed and also possible is the UK education system. Schools, colleges and universities are required to demonstrate inclusion, meaning that social justice and equity are being taken seriously. These are public institutions that need to be held accountable for their practices; they need to demonstrate that they are implementing policies with concrete outcomes that improve inclusion for black and minority ethnic staff and students.

Our education systems must firstly acknowledge institutional racism and white privilege; a failure to acknowledge racism results in a failure to act upon it and to instigate change. There is a need for specific institutional frameworks that facilitate change at local and national levels. Schools and universities, for example, must demonstrate a clear monitoring of racist incidents; this includes identifying measures which outline how racism is addressed through clear action plans with specific outcomes. This information should be communicated to education departments in order that clear strategies are in place for how educational institutions are addressing racism. As discussed in Chapter Seven, there is evidence to suggest that when complaints of racism are made in schools and universities, these complaints are often dismissed either as bad behaviour or a clash of personalities. Complaining about racism often results in the victims becoming labelled as the villains.

Universities should take the bold step to introduce unconscious bias training as mandatory for all staff; *at the very least* this training should be a requirement for individuals involved in promotion and recruitment panels. A greater visibility of black and minority ethnic staff is needed in senior decision–making roles so that there is a specific recognition and valuing of diversity in staff representation, as well as a diverse curriculum for students. Universities should be held to account for their lack of representation of black and minority ethnic groups in these roles. Clearly institutions can identify lack of representation – they are already implementing regular and systematic analysis of staff profiles, from which a wealth of data (age, gender, ethnicity, under [and over] representation, staff levels and type of contract, promotion and progression) can be gathered – and yet they cannot rectify it. In order to support black and minority ethnic staff to reach their full potential, all universities should be expected to provide formal mentoring and training to staff who wish to progress in their careers; such mentoring and training should be designed to address the specific needs of BME staff.

As discussed previously in Chapter Six, I have suggested that despite advances in policy making in higher education, this has resulted in little change to the inclusion of black and minority ethnic groups in senior roles. For example, whilst the Race Equality Charter is a positive move in the right direction, it is far too early to tell if it will make a difference to universities addressing racial inequalities. However, if it was directly linked to funding, and capping student fee-increases based on successful completion of the Charter, it might encourage a greater number of universities to apply for the award and directly address issues of racial inequality. In order for universities to be awarded funding from the research councils, they should demonstrate how they are addressing issues of race, equality and inclusion. Furthermore, universities must think about how they are addressing diversity. It is not enough for universities to say that they are addressing diversity because they have a high number of international students.

Universities continue to fail to address the racial make-up of their student bodies. Oxbridge and Russell Group universities still fail to recruit sufficient numbers of black and minority ethnic students. During the final stages of writing this book, Oxford University was accused of 'social apartheid' because nearly one in three colleges failed to admit even one black student in 2015.[1] Realistically, how can this be the case? Not *one* single black student was offered a place to study at Oxford in nearly one of three colleges in 2015? There is also evidence to suggest that Oxbridge recruits the richest in our society (83% of offers from Oxford and 81% of offers from Cambridge went to students from the top two socio-economic groups in 2015[2]); this further disadvantages black and minority ethnic groups as BME groups are more likely to be living in poverty compared to other groups (see Chapter Nine). What does this tell us about our education system? Possibly that what 'elite universities' stand for is less about intellectual and academic value and more about privilege, wealth and power.

I suggest that the UK government develops a specific policy that addresses inequalities in the application process by introducing name-blind applications for universities. There is ample evidence to suggest that job applicants with non-Eurocentric names are disadvantaged in securing interviews, and this may also be the case when students apply for different universities. Introducing name-blind applications would address implicit bias in the university application process. This would ensure a level playing-field for all applicants; they would be judged on the *quality* of their applications rather than a form of implicit bias based on their names.

I have discussed in Chapter Six how advantage is awarded to those already advantaged. Children from independent schools are more likely to gain a place at Oxbridge or a Russell Group university, yet only 6% of children in the UK attend independent schools. White privilege is awarded to those who are already privileged; it reinforces and perpetuates a system in which white elites maintain and reinforce their position of power at all levels. From the earliest age, from the day a child first steps into a reception class, schooling, higher education and then the labour market reinforces the same patterns of inequality. If we believe that education is a *right and not a privilege* then every individual, regardless of their race, gender or socio-economic background, has a right to a quality education. Universities must be held accountable for their actions and for failing to admit a diverse body of students. I suggest a specific policy be introduced to address this inequality: a quota system for elite universities such as Oxbridge and those in the Russell Group. These universities must admit a percentage of students from black and minority ethnic backgrounds per year. They must develop outreach programmes that target poor areas and under-performing schools. Students from these schools and areas should then be given support to develop their university applications, as well as training for interviews. The most successful students should then be awarded bursaries and scholarships. This is not a lowering of standards; in fact an inclusive approach would raise standards at these institutions. The brightest students are not currently entering Oxbridge; rather these universities select the brightest students in small cohorts, defined largely by race and class. Outreach programmes have been in place in Ivy League universities in the US for some time; this is why in 2017, for the first time in its history, more than half of Harvard's intake will not be white.[3] A similar quota system should also be introduced for black and minority ethnic students wishing to pursue postgraduate research degrees (PhD). I have discussed in Chapter Six how black and minority ethnic groups are less likely to continue to study for postgraduate research degrees compared to white and international students, due to lack of access to financial and economic capital. Introducing a quota system and bursaries and scholarships for the brightest students would ensure that BME students access postgraduate research degrees based on their *ability* rather than their access to financial and economic capital.

In this book I have argued that race continues to remain a disadvantage for those from black and minority ethnic groups in all walks of life. By virtue of their non-white identity, BME groups continue to be positioned as outsiders and remain marginalised in all aspects of society. Policy making within a neoliberal context, despite its attempts to create a society based on inclusive practice, has not only failed but *reinforced* inequalities between BME groups and white members of society. These inequalities stem from racist and exclusionary practices that continue to perpetuate white privilege and white dominance. Consequently, the image of a post-racial society remains a myth. As Myers and Bhopal suggest, 'To argue that post-Macpherson has resulted in a post-racial society is utterly absurd. Such discourses serve only to further disadvantage and marginalise black and minority ethnic communities. Racism exists at every level of society; it permeates our schools, our colleges and our universities. It is alive in all elements of society, our popular culture, our media, and the social spaces that we occupy'.[4]

In this book, I have argued that within a neoliberal context, policy making is legitimised through a rhetoric that reinforces the benefits of neoliberalism as a universal value, whilst evidentially it is clear such policy reinforces *whiteness* and *white privilege*. Policy making fails to acknowledge the role that race and inequality play in perpetuating advantage over disadvantage. Neoliberalism does not benefit *all* members of society equally. We do not live in a post-racial society. Instead race remains central to the judgements and values made about who is *deserving* and who is *undeserving*: who belongs and who does not. Race acts as a marker of difference in a society poisoned by fear, insecurity and instability. Consequently, 'others' and 'outsiders' remain easy targets for those who 'want their country back' or want to 'make America great again'. Whiteness and white privilege continues to dominate, with white groups doing everything within their overwhelming power to protect and perpetuate their own positions and status.

Notes

Chapter One

1 Olssen, 2000.
2 https://educatorvoices.wordpress.com/2013/05/22/what-have-schools-got-to-do-with-neo-liberalism/
3 I am aware of the complexities and limitations of the term 'black and minority ethnic', which I use throughout to refer to those from Black British, Black African, British Indian, Pakistani, Bangladeshi, and Chinese backgrounds, as well as those from other non-white backgrounds, but I have used it because it is the term used in the census and the one most commonly used in UK policy documents.
4 Robertson, 2005: 13.
5 Robertson, 2005: 2.
6 UNDP, 2005.
7 Davies and Bansel, 2007: 3.
8 Davies and Bansel, 2007: 4; see also Saul, 2005.
9 Goldberg, 2009.
10 *Revised Prevent Duty Guidance for England and Wales* (2015). London: HMI.
11 'Gypsy' and 'Traveller' are both difficult and contested terms. I use these terms in this book both to reflect the self-ascription of respondents in the studies described and also to reflect the terminology used in UK policy contexts.

Chapter Two

1 Equality and Human Rights Commission (EHRC), 2016.
2 EHRC, 2016.
3 EHRC, 2016.
4 http://blackdemographics.com/
5 http://blackdemographics.com/
6 BBC News 2016a.
7 *The Guardian*, 2016d.
8 *The Guardian*, 2016e.
9 *The Guardian*, 2016e.
10 *The Guardian*, 2016d.
11 http://lordashcroftpolls.com/2016/06//how-the-united-kingdom-voted-and-why

12 *The Guardian*, 2015b.
13 *The Guardian*, 2015b.
14 *The Guardian*, 2015b.
15 *Huffington Post*, 2016a.
16 http://blacklivesmatter.com/about/
17 http://blacklivesmatter.com/about/
18 Fox News, 2016.
19 BBC News, 2016b.
20 *The Guardian*, 2016f.
21 *Washington Post*, 2015.
22 *Huffington Post*, 2016b.
23 https://www.washingtonpost.com/news/post-politics/wp/2015/12/07/
    donald-trump-calls-for-total-and-complete-shutdown-of-muslims-
    entering-the-united-states/?utm_term=.0c1873a732a5
24 Newsday, 2016.
25 *The Atlantic*, 2016.
26 *Huffington Post*, 2016b.
27 Roediger, 2005.
28 Leonardo, 2009.
29 Taylor, 2000: 541.
30 Harris, 1993: 1724.
31 Bell, 1989.
32 http://code.ucsd.edu/pcosman/Backpack.pdf
33 McIntosh, 1989.
34 McIntosh, 1989.
35 Frankenberg, 1993.
36 Sleeter, 2011.
37 Sleeter, 2011: 424.
38 Roediger, 1999.
39 Sleeter, 2011: 430.
40 Marx and Pennington, 2010.
41 Helms, 1990.
42 Sleeter, 2011: 167.
43 Marx and Pennington, 2010.
44 Warikoo, 2016.
45 Rothstein, 2014.
46 McIntyre, 1997.
47 Riggins, 2001: 1.
48 Bonilla-Silva and Lewis, 1999.
49 Bonilla-Silva and Forman, 2000: 52.
50 https://www.vox.com/2016/5/25/11682950/fisher-supreme-court-
    white-women-affirmative-action
51 Bonilla-Silva and Forman, 2000: 78.
52 Morrison, 1993.

53 Garner, 2007.
54 Bonnett, 2000.
55 Roediger, 2005.
56 Preston, 2008: 476.
57 Bonnett, 2000.
58 Garner, 2012: 5.
59 Gillborn, 2005: 56.
60 Gillborn, 2012: 58.

Chapter Three

1 The Equality Act, 2010.
2 Office for National Statistics (ONS), 2014b.
3 ONS, 2014b.
4 ONS, 2014b.
5 ONS, 2014b.
6 EHRC, 2016.
7 EHRC, 2016.
8 Clark, 2014.
9 Department for Communities and Local Government (DCLG), 2016.
10 United Nations Human Rights Council (UNHRC), 2013.
11 EHRC, 2016.
12 EHRC, 2016; ONS, 2014b.
13 EHRC, 2016: 33.
14 Royal College of General Practitioners (RCGP), 2013.
15 HM Inspectorate of Prisons (HMIP), 2014.
16 EHRC, 2016.
17 EHRC, 2016: 49.
18 http://www.theguardian.com/media/2012/oct/16/big-fat-gypsy-weddings-bullying-travellers
19 http://eur-lex.europa.eu/legal-content/EN/TXT/?qid=1444909812175&uri=CELEX:52010DC0133
20 http://eur-lex.europa.eu/legal-content/EN/TXT/?qid=1444909812175&uri=CELEX:52010DC0133
21 http://eur-lex.europa.eu/legal-content/EN/TXT/?qid=1444910104414&uri=CELEX:52011DC0173
22 European Union (EU), 2015: 14.
23 Osler, 2016: 143.
24 Quality Curriculum Agency (QCA), 1998.
25 Department for Children Schools and Families (DCSF), 2008; Osler and Starkey, 2010.
26 Bhopal and Myers, 2009.
27 Department for Education (DfE), 2015c.
28 DCSF, 2008: 4.
29 Bhopal et al, 2000.
30 National Union of Teachers (NUT), 2011.

31 Irish Traveller Movement, 2011: 8.
32 DCSF, 2010; Myers and Bhopal, 2015.
33 Bhopal and Myers, 2016.
34 Bhopal and Myers, 2017.
35 Myers and Bhopal, 2015.
36 Bhopal and Myers, 2016.
37 DES, 2003: 3.
38 EHRC, 2016.
39 Myers et al, 2010.

Chapter Four

1 Crenshaw, 1989.
2 Crenshaw, 1989: 1243.
3 Crenshaw, 1991: 1252.
4 Crenshaw, 1989: 140.
5 Beck, 1992.
6 Washington, 1987.
7 Bell, 1995: 901.
8 Bell, 1995: 902.
9 Brah, 1996; Anthias and Yuval-Davis, 1992.
10 Lewis, 2000.
11 Brah, 1996.
12 Brah, 1996: 208.
13 Preston and Bhopal, 2011.
14 Preston and Bhopal, 2011: 219.
15 Equality Challenge Unit (ECU), 2016a.
16 ECU, 2016b.
17 ECU, 2016b.
18 Research Councils UK, http://www.rcuk.ac.uk/funding/diversity/
19 Macdonald, 2014.
20 http://www.ecu.ac.uk/equality-charters/race-equality-charter/
21 ECU, 2016c.
22 ECU, 2016c.
23 ECU, 2013: 1.
24 ECU, 2013: 1.
25 Carlsson and Rooth, 2008; Moss-Racusin et al, 2012.
26 Dobin and Kalev, 2016.
27 ECU, 2013: 7.
28 Kings College London, 2016.
29 Pilkington, 2013.
30 Equality Act Guidance, 2010.
31 Census, 2011.
32 ECU, 2015a.
33 ECU, 2015a.
34 Bhopal, 2016.

35 Bhopal, Brown and Jackson, 2015.
36 Post-1992 universities were former polytechnics which were given university status after the 1992 Further and Higher Education Act (UK). They are teaching rather than research focussed.
37 Sue et al, 2007: 273.

Chapter Five

1 Swann Report, 1985.
2 Alexander et al, 2015: 4.
3 Race Relations Amendment Act, 2000.
4 Macpherson, 1999.
5 Equality Act, 2010.
6 DfE, 2014b: 30.
7 DfE, 2014b: 30.
8 DfE, 2015b.
9 DfE, 2015b.
10 DfE, 2015c.
11 DfE, 2015c.
12 Weekes-Bernard, 2007.
13 Race on the Agenda, 2012.
14 Equality Act, 2010.
15 Race on the Agenda, 2012.
16 DfE, 2015c.
17 EHRC, 2016: 18; DfE, 2015b.
18 Ditch the Label, 2015.
19 UNCRC, 2008.
20 Gutnam and Vorhaus, 2012.
21 Lereya et al, 2013.
22 EHRC, 2016.
23 OFSTED, 2012.
24 NSPCC, 2014.
25 Estyn, 2014.
26 Dennell and Logan, 2015.
27 DfE, 2014a: 4.
28 DfE, 2014a: 5.
29 DfE, 2014a: 7.
30 BBC News, 2015.
31 BBC News, 2015.
32 Daily Mail Online, 2014.
33 *The Telegraph*, 2016.
34 *The Telegraph*, 2016.
35 *The Telegraph*, 2016.
36 Daily Mail Online, 2016.
37 DfE, 2013: 3.
38 DfE, 2013: 1.
39 DfE, 2015c: 7.

40 DfE, 2015c: 5.
41 Crozier, 2015: 36.
42 Horgan, 2014.
43 Wheatstone, 2015.
44 *The Guardian*, 2016b.
45 Independent Reviewer of Terrorism Legislation, 2016.
46 *The Guardian*, 2015a.
47 Carter, 2003.
48 Weekes-Bernard, 2007.
49 Gillborn, 2008.
50 Solomon et al, 2005.
51 Bhopal and Rhamie, 2014.
52 Kohli, 2014; Pearce, 2014.
53 Doharty, 2015.
54 Doharty, 2015: 54.
55 Alexander et al, 2012.
56 Crozier, 2015: 39.
57 https://nces.ed.gov/programs/coe/indicator_coi.asp
58 https://nces.ed.gov/programs/coe/indicator_cnc.asp
59 https://nces.ed.gov/programs/coe/indicator_cnb.asp
60 *The Guardian*, 2016c.
61 US News, 2016.
62 Skiba et al, 2002.
63 Lipman, 2012.
64 Milner et al, 2013.
65 McGee and Martin, 2011.
66 BBC World News, 2015.
67 Reay, 2005.

Chapter Six

1   Russell Group universities consist of a group of 24 leading research-intensive universities in the UK which are ranked highly in league tables.
2   ECU, 2015b.
3   ECU, 2015b.
4   ECU, 2015b.
5   ECU, 2015b.
6   ECU, 2015b.
7   ECU, 2015b.
8   ECU, 2015b.
9   ECU, 2015b.
10 ECU, 2015b.
11 ECU, 2015b.
12 ECU, 2015b.
13 ECU, 2015b.

[14] MillionPlus is the association of modern universities which focus on promoting research and teaching through widening participation agendas.

[15] ECU, 2015b.

[16] Runnymede Trust, 2010.

[17] ECU, 2015b.

[18] Department for Education and Skills (DfES) Widening Participation Agenda, 1999.

[19] ISC Census and annual report 2017, https://www.isc.co.uk/media/4069/isc-census-2017-final.pdf

[20] Sutton Trust, 2014.

[21] Reay, 2015: 15.

[22] Reay, 2015: 20.

[23] Reay, 2015: 20.

[24] Social Mobility and Child Poverty Commission, 2015: 94.

[25] Social Mobility and Child Poverty Commission, 2015: 8.

[26] Social Mobility and Child Poverty Commission, 2015: 8.

[27] Boliver, 2015.

[28] Business Innovation and Skills (BIS), 2013.

[29] 'A' levels are advanced level public examinations taken by students in England at age 18 for entrance into university.

[30] Boliver, 2015: 15; see also Noden et al 2014; Parel and Boliver, 2014.

[31] Boliver, 2015.

[32] Boliver, 2015: 15–16.

[33] Noden et al, 2014.

[34] Boliver, 2015: 16.

[35] Times Higher Education, 2016c.

[36] Times Higher Education, 2016b.

[37] Times Higher Education, 2016b.

[38] Burke, 2015: 21.

[39] Burke, 2015: 22.

[40] Burke, 2015: 22.

[41] National Union of Students, 2011.

[42] Bouattia, 2015.

[43] Bouattia, 2015: 26.

[44] Loke, 2015: 42.

[45] Higher Education Statistics Agency (HESA), 2014.

[46] Universities UK, 2013a.

[47] Universities UK, 2013b.

[48] Morgan, 2011.

[49] Higher Education Funding Council for England (HEFCE), 2016.

[50] HEFCE, 2016.

[51] http://www.hefce.ac.uk/pubs/year/2016/201614/

[52] Bhopal, 2018 in press.

[53] HEFCE, 2016: 19.

[54] Times Higher Education, 2016a.

[55] National Union of Students Connect, 2016.

56 *The Guardian*, 2016a; see also http://www.consented.co.uk/read/is-it-possible-to-decolonize-british-universities/
57 National Centre for Education Statistics (NCES), 2016.
58 NCES, 2016.
59 NCES, 2016.
60 NCES, 2016.
61 NCES, 2016.
62 Warikoo, 2016.
63 Karabel, 2005: 5.
64 Stevens, 2007.
65 Warikoo, 2016: 18.
66 Quillian, 2006.
67 Sears and Henry, 2003.
68 Small et al, 2010.
69 Kinder and Sanders, 1996: 223.
70 Lowery et al, 2006.
71 Warikoo, 2016: 104.
72 Warikoo, 2016: 104.
73 Warikoo, 2016: 111.
74 Reardon et al, 2012.
75 Bonilla–Silva, 2012.
76 Bonilla–Silva, 2003: 9; see also Gillborn, 2005.
77 Warikoo, 2016: 138; see also Hunt, 2007.
78 Jackman and Muha, 1984.
79 Reardon et al, 2012.
80 Alon, 2009.
81 Reardon et al, 2012.
82 Warikoo, 2016.

Chapter Seven

1 DfE, 2014a: 2.
2 DfE, 2014a: 4.
3 DfE, 2014a: 5.
4 DfE, 2014a: 7.
5 DfE, 2014a.
6 https://www.gov.uk/bullying-at-school/bullying-a-definition
7 BBC News, 2012.
8 BBC News, 2012.
9 Bhopal and Myers, 2016.
10 Trades Union Congress (TUC), 2013: 3.
11 TUC, 2013: 11.
12 TUC, 2013: 12.
13 *The Independent*, 2014.
14 NSPCC, 2015.
15 *The Independent*, 2016.

16 ECU, 2015a: 50.
17 ECU, 2015a.
18 University and College Union (UCU), 2016: 1.
19 UCU, 2016.
20 UCU, 2016: 12.
21 UCU, 2016: 13.
22 ECU, 2015a.
23 ECU, 2015a.
24 National Student Survey (NSS), 2014.
25 Bell and Brooks, 2016.
26 Bell and Brooks, 2016: 18.
27 Times Higher Education, 2016a.
28 Concrete, 2016.
29 OFSTED is The Office for Standards in Education, Children's Services and Skills, and inspects and regulates services that care for children and young people, and services that provide education.
30 Bhopal, 2014: 3.
31 Bhopal, 2014: 3.
32 Bonilla-Silva and Forman, 2000: 78.
33 Özbilgin and Tatli, 2011: 1245.
34 Bhopal and Myers, 2016: 17.

Chapter Eight

1 Morgan, 2014.
2 Universities UK, 2013a.
3 HEFCE, 2016.
4 Catney and Sabater, 2015.
5 ONS, 2015.
6 ONS, 2015.
7 ONS, 2015.
8 ONS, 2015.
9 ONS, 2015.
10 ONS, 2015.
11 ONS, 2015.
12 EHRC, 2016.
13 EHRC, 2016: 21.
14 EHRC, 2016: 21.
15 Hills et al, 2015.
16 EHRC, 2016.
17 Trades Union Congress (TUC), 2015.
18 Catney and Sabater, 2015, Vizard et al, 2015.
19 EHRC, 2016: 23.
20 EHRC, 2016.
21 EHRC, 2016: 24; Green Park, 2015.
22 National Audit Office (NAO), 2015.

[23] EHRC, 2016: 25.
[24] EHRC, 2016: 25.
[25] TUC, 2016.
[26] EHRC, 2016: 25; TUC, 2016.
[27] EHRC, 2016: 25.
[28] EHRC, 2016; Zwysen and Longhi, 2016.
[29] Boliver, 2016; Richardson, 2015.
[30] Colding et al, 2009.
[31] Lindley, 2009.
[32] Rafferty, 2012.
[33] Kadushin, 2012.
[34] Zuccotti, 2015.
[35] Zwysen and Longhi, 2016.
[36] Li, 2015.
[37] Li, 2015: 25.
[38] Li, 2015: 26.
[39] Patacchini and Zenou, 2011.
[40] Abreu et al, 2014.
[41] Feng et al, 2015.
[42] Zwysen and Longhi, 2016: 12; Holzer, 1988.
[43] Zwysen and Longhi, 2016: 33.
[44] Zwysen and Longhi, 2016: 34.
[45] Catney and Sabater, 2015: 8.
[46] Catney and Sabater, 2015: 9.
[47] Catney and Sabater, 2015: 10.
[48] Catney and Sabater, 2015.
[49] Heath and Cheung, 2007; Bourn, 2008.
[50] Catney and Sabater, 2015: 12.
[51] Fieldhouse, 1999.
[52] Catney and Sabater, 2015: 12.
[53] Owen, 2013.
[54] Simpson et al, 2006.
[55] Hudson and Radu, 2011.
[56] Jones and Ram, 2007.
[57] Catney and Sabater, 2015: 7.
[58] Catney and Sabater, 2015.
[59] Brynin and Guveli, 2012.
[60] EHRC, 2016.
[61] Catney and Sabater, 2015.
[62] Bourn, 2008.
[63] Catney and Sabater, 2015: 15.
[64] Catney and Sabater, 2015.
[65] Catney and Sabater, 2015: 22.
[66] Longhi et al, 2013.
[67] Catney and Sabater, 2015: 77.
[68] Catney and Sabater, 2015: 77; Bauder, 2001.

[69] TUC, 2016.
[70] Civil Service, 2015: 4.
[71] Department for Work and Pensions (DWP), 2016: 3.
[72] DWP, 2016.
[73] TUC, 2016.

Chapter Nine

[1] Catney and Sabater, 2015.
[2] Barnard, 2014.
[3] Harkness et al, 2012.
[4] Lalani et al, 2014.
[5] Catney and Sabater, 2015: 12.
[6] Menash, 1995.
[7] Holtom et al, 2013.
[8] Lalani et al, 2014.
[9] Catney and Sabater, 2015.
[10] Hills et al, 2013
[11] Catney and Sabater, 2015.
[12] EHRC, 2016.
[13] EHRC, 2016.
[14] EHRC, 2016.
[15] EHRC, 2016.
[16] EHRC, 2016.
[17] EHRC, 2016: 28.
[18] EHRC, 2016.
[19] EHRC, 2016: 30.
[20] Runnymede Trust, 2015.
[21] Joseph Rowntree Foundation, 2016.
[22] Fisher and Nandi, 2015.
[23] Fisher and Nandi, 2015.
[24] Jivraj and Khan, 2013: 1.
[25] Jivraj and Khan, 2013.
[26] Fisher and Nandi, 2015.
[27] EHRC, 2016.
[28] EHRC, 2016: 30.
[29] EHRC, 2016: 30.
[30] Health and Social Care Information Centre (HSCIC), 2015.
[31] EHRC, 2016.
[32] EHRC, 2016: 34.
[33] US Census Bureau, 2014.
[34] Black Demographics, 2016.
[35] Black Demographics, 2016.
[36] http://npc.umich.edu/poverty/
[37] http://npc.umich.edu/poverty/
[38] http://www.nccp.org/publications/pub_1145.html
[39] Jiang et al, 2016.

40 Yumiko, 2009.
41 Jiang et al, 2016: 6.
42 Jiang et al, 2016.
43 Jargowsky, 2015: 2.
44 Jargowsky, 2015: 2.
45 Jargowsky, 2015: 13.
46 Jargowsky, 2015: 15.
47 Berkeley News, 2014.
48 Berkeley News, 2014.
49 Berkeley News, 2014.
50 Pew Research, 2015.
51 Newsweek Europe, 2015.

Chapter Ten

1 https://www.theguardian.com/education/2017/oct/19/oxford-accused-of-social-apartheid-as-colleges-admit-no-black-students
2 https://www.theguardian.com/education/2017/oct/19/oxbridge-becoming-less-diverse-as-richest-gain-80-of-offers
3 http://www.bbc.co.uk/news/world-us-canada-40812196
4 Myers and Bhopal, 2015: 140.

References

Abreu, M., Faggian, A. and McCann, P. (2014) 'Migration and inter-industry mobility of UK graduates', *Journal of Economic Geography* 15(2): 353-85.

Alexander, C., Chatterji, J. and Weekes-Bernard, D. (2012) *Making British Histories: Diversity and the National Curriculum*, London: The Runnymede Trust.

Alexander, C., Arday, J. and Weekes-Bernard, D. (2015) *Race, Education and Inequality in Contemporary Britain*, London: The Runnymede Trust.

Alon, S. (2009) 'The evolution of class inequality in higher education: competition, exclusion and adaptation', *American Sociological Review* 74(5): 731–55.

Anthias, F. and Yuval-Davis, N. (1992) *Racialised Boundaries – Race, Nation, Gender, Colour and Class and the Anti-Racist Struggle*, London: Routledge.

The Atlantic (2016) 'Donald Trump's coalition of restoration', 23 June, http://www.theatlantic.com/politics/archive/2016/06/donald-trumps-coalition-of-restoration/488345/.

Barnard, H. (2014) *Tackling Poverty Across All Ethnicities in the UK*, York: Joseph Rowntree Foundation.

Bauder, H. (2001) 'Culture in the labor market: segmentation theory and perspectives of place', *Progress in Human Geography* 25(1): 37–52.

BBC News (2012) 'More than 87,000 racist incidents recorded at schools', 23 May, http://www.bbc.co.uk/news/education-18155255.

BBC News (2015) 'Trojan Horse schools plotline', 16 July, http://www.bbc.co.uk.news/education-31905704.

BBC News (2016a) '"Racist" graffiti on Polish cultural centre in London', 26 June, http://www.bbc.co.uk/news/uk-england-london-36634621.

BBC News (2016b) "'Don't shoot!" Wife tells Carolina Police', 24 September, http://www.bbc.co.uk/news/world-us-canada-37456727.

BBC World News (2015) 'How do black students perform at school?', 29 May, http://www.bbc.co.uk/news/world-us-canada-32824482.

Beck, U. (1992) *Risk Society: Towards a New Modernity*, London: Sage.

Bell, B. and Brooks, C. (2016) *Analysis of NSS Teaching Scores*, Reading: University of Reading Research Report.

Bell, D. (1995) 'Who's afraid of critical race theory?' *University of Illinois Law Review* 4: 893–910.

Bell, E. (1989) *Slaves in the Family*, New York: Ballantine.

Berkeley News (2014) 'Greater income inequality linked to more deaths for Black African Americans', 1 December, http://news.berkeley.edu/2014/12/01/income-inequality-higher-mortality/.

Bhopal, K. (2014) *The Experiences of BME Academics in Higher Education: Aspirations in the Face of Inequality*, London: LFHE.

Bhopal, K. (2016) *The Experiences of Black and Minority Ethnic Academics: A Comparative Study of the Unequal Academy*, London: Routledge.

Bhopal, K. (2018 in press) *The Transitions Study: Undergraduate Student Choices*, Birmingham: University of Birmingham Project Report.

Bhopal, K. and Myers, M. (2009) 'Gypsy, Roma and Traveller pupils in schools in the UK: inclusion and good practice', *International Journal of Inclusive Education* 13(3): 219–31.

Bhopal, K. and Myers, M. (2016) 'Marginal groups in marginal times: Gypsy and Traveller parents and home education in England, UK', *British Educational Research Journal* 42(1): 5–20.

Bhopal, K. and Myers, M. (2017) *Education, Risk and Marginal Groups*. Paper presented at annual ECER Conference, Copenhagen, August.

Bhopal, K. and Rhamie, J. (2014) 'Initial teacher training: understanding "race", diversity and inclusion', *Race, Ethnicity and Education* 17(3): 304–25.

Bhopal, K., Brown, H. and Jackson, J. (2015) *Academic Flight: How to Encourage BME Academics to Stay in UK Higher Education*, London: ECU.

Bhopal, K., Gundara, J., Jones, C. and Owen, C. (2000) *Working Towards Inclusive Education: Aspects of Good Practice*, London: DfEE.

Black Demographics (2016) http://blackdemographics.com/households/poverty/.

Black Lives Matter (2016) http://blacklivesmatter.com/about/.

Boliver, V. (2015) 'Why are ethnic minorities less likely to be offered places at selective universities?', in C. Alexander and J. Arday (eds), *Aiming Higher: Race, Inequality and Diversity in Higher Education*, London: Runnymede, pp 15–19.

Boliver, V. (2016) 'Exploring ethnic inequalities in admission to Russell Group universities', *Sociology* 50(2): 247–66.

Bonilla-Silva, E. (2003) *Racism without Racists: Color Blind Racism and the Persistence of Racial Inequality in the United States*, Lanham, MD: Rowman and Littlefield.

Bonilla-Silva, E. (2012) 'The invisible weight of whiteness', *Ethnic and Racial Studies* 25(2): 173–94.

Bonilla-Silva, E. and Lewis, A. (1999) 'The new racism: racial structure in the United States, 1960s–1990s', in P. Wong (ed), *Race, Ethnicity, and Nationality in the United States: Toward the Twenty-First Century*, Boulder, CO: Westview Press, pp 55–101.

Bonilla-Silva, E. and Forman, T. (2000) '"I am not a racist but ...": mapping white college students' ideology in the USA', *Discourse and Society* 11(1): 50–85.

Bonnett, A. (2000) *White Identities: Historical and International Perspectives*, London: Prentice Hall.

Bouattia, M. (2015) 'Beyond the gap: dismantling institutional racism, decolonising education', in C. Alexander and J. Arday (eds), *Aiming Higher: Race, Inequality and Diversity in Higher Education*, London: Runnymede, pp 24–7.

Bourn, J. (2008) *Increasing Employment Rates for Ethnic Minorities: A Report by the Controller and Auditor General*, London: The Stationery Office, http://www.nao.org.uk/report/increasing-employment-rates-for-ethnic-minorities/.

Brah, A. (1996) *Cartographies of Diaspora: Contesting Identities*, London: Routledge.

Brynin, M. and Guveli, A. (2012) 'Understanding the ethnic pay gap in Britain', *Work, Employment and Society* 26(4): 574–87.

Burke, P. (2015) 'Widening participation in higher education: racialised inequalities and misrecognitions', in C. Alexander and J. Arday (eds), *Aiming Higher: Race, Inequality and Diversity in Higher Education*, London: Runnymede, pp 21–4.

Business Innovation and Skills (BIS) (2013) *Investigating the Accuracy of Predicted A level Grades as Part of the 2010 UCAS Admissions Process, Research Paper No. 20*, London: Department for Business, Innovation and Skills.

Carlsson, M. and Rooth, D. (2008) *Is It Your Foreign Name or Foreign Qualifications? An Experimental Study of Ethnic Discrimination in Hiring*, Bonn: Institute for the Study of Labour.

Carter, P. (2003) '"Black" cultural capital, status positioning, and schooling conflicts for low-income African American youth', *Social Problems* 50(1): 136–55.

Catney, G. and Sabater, A. (2015) *Ethnic Minority Disadvantage in the Labour Market*, London: Joseph Rowntree Foundation.

Census (2011) Office for National Statistics: London.

Civil Service (2015) *Ethnic Dimension: Identifying and Removing Barriers to Talented BME Staff Progression in the Civil Service*, London: The Stationery Office.

Clark, K. (2014) *Is the Picture of Pakistani Self-employment Really So Cosy?* Manchester Policy Blogs, Manchester University.

Colding, B., Husted, L. and Hummelgaard, H. (2009) 'Educational progression of second-generation immigrants and immigrant children', *Economic Educational Review* 28: 434–43.

Concrete (2016) 'Survey reveals bias against BME academics', 20 January, http://www.concrete-online.co.uk/survey-reveals-student-bias-against-bme-academics/.

Crenshaw, K. (1989) 'De-marginalising the intersection of race and sex', *University of Chicago Legal Forum* 139: 139–67.

Crenshaw, K. (1991) 'Mapping the margins: intersectionality, identity politics, and violence against women of color', *Stanford Law Review* 43(6): 1241–99.

Crozier, G. (2015) 'Black and minority ethnic students on the margins: self-segregation or enforced exclusion', in C. Alexander, J. Arday and D. Weekes-Bernard (eds), *Race, Education and Inequality in Contemporary Britain*, London: Runnymede, pp 36–9.

Daily Mail Online (2014) 'British values aren't optional, they're vital', 15 June, http://www.dailymail.co.uk/debate/article-2658171/DAVID-CAMERON-British-values-arent-optional-theyre-vital-Thats-I-promote-EVERY-school-As-row-rages-Trojan-Horse-takeover-classrooms-Prime-Minister-delivers-uncompromising-pledge.html#ixzz4MIfYA0Zw.

Daily Mail Online (2016) 'Militant teachers demand schools stop promoting British values as it makes children from other cultures feel inferior', 28 March, http://www.dailymail.co.uk/news/article-3512619/Teachers-want-stop-promoting-British-values-cultural-supremacy-fears.html.

Davies, B. and Bansel, P. (2007) 'Neoliberalism and education', *International Journal of Qualitative Studies in Education* 20(3): 247–59.

Dennell, B. and Logan, B. (2015) *Tackling Bullying in Scotland's Schools*, Strathclyde: Public Policy Institute.

Department for Children, Schools and Families (2008) *National Strategies: Gypsy, Roma and Traveller Communities*, London: DCSF.

Department for Children, Schools and Families (2010) *Improving the Outcomes for Gypsy, Roma and Traveller Pupils*, London: DCSF.

Department for Communities and Local Government (2016) *Progress Made by the Ministerial Working Group on Tackling Inequalities Experienced by Gypsies and Travellers*, London: DCLG.

Department for Education (2013) *National Curriculum Key Stages 3 and 4*, London: DfE.

Department for Education (2014a) *The Equality Act and Schools*, London: DfE.

Department for Education (2014b) *Promoting Fundamental Values through SMSC*, London: DfE.

Department for Education (2015a) *GCSE and equivalent attainment by pupil characteristics, 2013 to 2014 (Revised)*, SFR06/2015, London: DfE.

Department for Education (2015b) *Prevent Guidance for Schools*, London: DfE.

Department for Education (2015c) 'Schools attendance and absence', https://www.gov.uk/school-attendance-absence/legal-action-to-enforce-school-attendance.

Department for Education and Science (DES) (2003) *Aiming High: Raising the Achievement of Gypsy and Roma Pupils*, London: DES.

Department for Education and Skills (DfES) Widening Participation Agenda (2004) 'Participation rates in higher education for the academic years 1999/2000–2002/2003', Department for Education and Skills first release, 14 April.

Department for Work and Pensions (2016) *Labour Market Status by Ethnic Group*, London: The Stationery Office.

Digest of Education Statistics 2015, table 306.50, https://nces.ed.gov/programs/digest/2015menu_tables.asp.

Ditch the Label (2015) *The Annual Bullying Survey*, London: Ditch the Label.

Dobin, F. and Kalev, A. (2016) 'Why diversity programs fail', *Harvard Business Review* (July–August).

Doharty, N. (2015) 'Hard time pressure in Babylon: why Black History in schools is failing to meet the needs of BME students at Key Stage 3', in C. Alexander, J. Arday and D. Weekes-Bernard (eds), *Race, Education and Inequality in Contemporary Britain*, London: Runnymede, pp 51–5.

Equality Act (2010) https://www.gov.uk/guidance/equality-act-2010-guidance.

Equality Challenge Unit (2013) *Unconscious Bias and Higher Education*, London: ECU.

Equality Challenge Unit (2015a) *Statistical Report: Staff*, London: ECU.

Equality Challenge Unit (2015b) *Equality in Higher Education, Part 2: Students*, London: ECU.

Equality Challenge Unit (2016a) 'Who we are', http://www.ecu.ac.uk/about-us/who-we-are/.

Equality Challenge Unit (2016b) 'Athena Swan Charter', http://www.ecu.ac.uk/equality-charters/athena-swan/about-athena-swan/.

Equality Challenge Unit (2016c) 'Race Equality Charter', http://www.ecu.ac.uk/equality-charters/race-equality-charter/about-race-equality-charter.

Equality and Human Rights Commission (2016) *Healing a Divided Britain: The Need for a Comprehensive Race Equality Strategy*, London: EHRC.

Estyn Excellence for all (2014) *Action on Bullying*, Wales: Her Majesty's Inspectorate in Wales.

European Union (2015) *Human Rights of Roma and Travellers in Europe*, Brussels: Council of Europe.

Feng, X., Flowerdew, R. and Feng, Z. (2015) 'Does neighbourhood influence ethnic inequalities in economic activity? Findings from the ONS Longitudinal Study', *Journal of Economic Geography* 15: 169–94.

Fieldhouse, E. (1999) 'Ethnic minority unemployment and spatial mismatch: the case of London', *Urban Studies* 36(9): 1569–96.

Fisher, P. and Nandi, A. (2015) *Poverty Across Ethnic Groups through Recession and Austerity*, York: Joseph Rowntree Foundation.

Fox News (2016) 'Milwaukee shooting was 23 year old black man', 14 August, http://www.foxnews.com/us/2016/08/14/mother-milwaukee-shooting-victim-was-23-year-old-black-man.html.

Frankenberg, R. (1993) *The Social Construction of Whiteness: White Women, Race Matters*, Minneapolis, MN: University of Minnesota Press.

Garner, S. (2007) *Whiteness: An Introduction*, Oxford: Routledge.

Garner, S. (2012) 'A moral economy of whiteness: behaviours, belonging and Britishness', *Ethnicities* 12(4): 1–19.

Gillborn, D. (2005) 'Education as an act of white supremacy: whiteness, Critical Race Theory and education reform', *Journal of Education Policy* 20: 485–505.

Gillborn, D. (2008) *Coincidence or Conspiracy?* London: Routledge.

Gillborn, D. (2012) 'The white working class, racism and respectability: victims, degenerates and interest-convergence', *British Journal of Educational Studies* 58(1): 3–25.

Goldberg, D. (2009) *The Threat of Race: Reflections on Neoliberalism*, Malden, MA: Blackwell.

Green Park (2015) 'New leadership 10,000 report', http://www.green-park.co.uk/new-leadership-10000-report.

The Guardian (2015a) 'Family of boy arrested over homemade clock sues Texas school officials', 8 August, https://www.theguardian.com/us-news/2016/aug/08/ahmed-mohamed-clock-texas-lawsuit.

The Guardian (2015b) 'Young black men killed by US police at highest rate in year at 1,134 deaths', 31 December, https://www.theguardian.com/us-news/2015/dec/31/the-counted-police-killings-2015-young-black-men.

The Guardian (2016a) 'The real meaning of Rhodes must fall', 16 March, https://www.theguardian.com/uk-news/2016/mar/16/the-real-meaning-of-rhodes-must-fall.

The Guardian (2016b) 'Prevent strategy could end up promoting extremism', 21 April, http://www.theguardian.com/politics/2016/apr/21/government-prevent-strategy-promoting-extremism-maina-kiai.

The Guardian (2016c) 'Black children in US nearly four times as likely to be suspended as white children', 8 June, https://www.theguardian.com/education/2016/jun/08/us-education-survey-race-student-suspensions-absenteeism.

The Guardian (2016d) 'After a campaign fuelled by bigotry, it's ok to be racist', 28 June, https://www.theguardian.com/commentisfree/2016/jun/28/campaign-bigotry-racist-britain-leave-brexit.

The Guardian (2016e) 'A frenzy of hatred: how to understand Brexit racism', 29 June, http://www.theguardian.com/politics/2016/jun/29/frenzy-hatred-brexit-racism-abuse-referendum-celebratory-lasting-damage.

The Guardian (2016f) 'Black lives matter and the Democratic Convention', 26 July, https://www.theguardian.com/us-news/2016/jul/26/black-lives-matter-mothers-democratic-convention-hillary-clinton.

Gutnam, L. and Vorhaus, J. (2012) *The Impact of Pupil Behaviour and Wellbeing on Educational Outcomes*, London: DfE.

Harkness, S., Gregg, P. and MacMillan, L. (2012) *Poverty: The Role of Institutions, Behaviours and Cultures*, York: Joseph Rowntree Foundation.

Harris, C. (1993) 'Whiteness as property', *Harvard Law Review* 106: 1707–91.

Heath, A. and Cheung, S. (2007) *Unequal Chances: Ethnic Minorities in Western Labour Markets*, Oxford: Oxford University Press.

Health and Social Care Information Centre (HSCIC) (2015) *Inpatients Formally Detained in Hospitals under the Mental Health Act*, London: HSCIC.

Helms, J. (1990) *Black and White Racial Identity: Theory, Research and Practice*, New York: Greenwood Books.

Higher Education Funding Council for England (2016) *Transitions into Post Graduate Study*, London: HEFCE.

Higher Education Statistics Agency (2014) *Higher Education Statistics for the UK, 2013/14 (Student Destinations)*, London: HESA.

Hills, J., Cunliffe, J., Gambaro, L. and Obolenskaya, P. (2013) *Winners and Losers in the Crisis: The Changing Anatomy of Inequality in the UK 2007–2010*, York and London: Joseph Rowntree and Nuffield Foundations.

Hills, J., Cunliffe, J., Obolenskaya, P. and Karagiannaki, E. (2015) 'Falling behind, getting ahead: the changing structure of inequality in the UK, 2007–2013', Social Policy in Cold Climate Research Paper No. 5, http://sticerd.lse.ac.uk/dps/case/spcc/rr05.pdf.

HM Inspectorate of Prisons (2014) *Report on an Unannounced Inspection of Harmondsworth Immigration Removal Centre*, London: HMIP.

Holtom, D., Bottril, I. and Watkins, J. (2013) *Poverty and Ethnicity in Wales*, York: Joseph Rowntree Foundation.

Holzer, H.J. (1988) 'Search method use by unemployed youth', *Journal of Labour Economics* 6: 1–20.

Horgan, J. (2014) *The Psychology of Terrorism*, London: Routledge.

Households Below Average Income (HBAI) (2016) Department for Work and Pensions, UK, http://www.jrf.org.uk/data/poverty-rate-ethnicity).

Hudson, M. and Radu, D. (2011) *The Role of Employer Attitudes and Behaviour*, York: Joseph Rowntree Foundation.

Huffington Post (2016a) 'More than 250 black people were killed by police in 2016', http://www.huffingtonpost.com/entry/black-people-killed-by-police-america_us_577da633e4b0c590f7e7fb17.

Huffington Post (2016b) '13 examples of Donald Trump being racist', 25 August, http://www.huffingtonpost.com/entry/donald-trump-racist-examples_us_56d47177e4b03260bf777e83.

Hunt, M. (2007) 'African American and Hispanic beliefs about Black/White inequality, 1977–2004', *American Sociological Review* 72(3): 390–415.

The Independent (2014) 'Racist bullying: "far right" agenda on immigration being taken into classrooms', 25 August, http://www.independent.co.uk/news/education/education-news/racist-bullying-far-right-agenda-on-immigration-being-taken-into-classrooms-9045148.html.

The Independent (2016) 'Surge of racist incidents in schools sees over 20 children excluded every day', 3 August, http://www.independent.co.uk/news/education/education-news/racism-schools-stats-children-excluded-per-day-rises-racist-incidents-a7178746.html.

Independent Reviewer of Terrorism Legislation (2016) https://terrorismlegislationreviewer.independent.gov.uk.

Irish Traveller Movement (2011) *Gypsy, Roma and Traveller Education: Improving Outcomes, Briefing*, London: Irish Traveller Movement in Britain.

ISC Census and annual report (2017) https://www.isc.co.uk/media/4069/isc-census-2017-final.pdf

Jackman, M. and Muha, M. (1984) 'Education and intergroup attitudes: moral enlightenment, superficial democratic commitment or ideological refinement?' *American Sociological Review* 49(6): 751–69.

Jargowsky, P. (2015) *The Architecture of Segregation*, New York: The Century Foundation.

Jiang, Y., Ekono, M.M. and Skinner, C. (2016) 'Basic facts about low-income children, children under 18 years, 2013', http://academiccommons.columbia.edu/catalog/ac:182940.

Jivraj, S. and Khan, O. (2013) 'Ethnicity and deprivation in England: how likely are ethnic minorities to live in deprived neighbourhoods? *Dynamics of Diversity: Evidence from the 2011 Census*, CoDE/JRF.

Jones, T. and Ram, M. (2007) 'Re-embedding the ethnic business agenda', *Work, Employment and Society* 21(3): 439–57.

Joseph Rowntree Foundation (2016) 'Poverty rate by ethnicity', 29 June, http://www.jrf.org.uk/data/poverty-rate-ethnicity.

Kadushin, C. (2012) *Understanding Social Networks*, Oxford: Oxford University Press.

Karabel, J. (2005) *The Chosen: The Hidden History of Admission and Exclusion at Harvard, Yale, and Princeton*, Boston, MA: Houghton Mifflin Harcourt.

Kinder, D. and Sanders, L. (1996) *Divided by Color: Racial Politics and Democratic Ideals, American Politics and Political Economy*, Chicago, IL: University of Chicago Press.

Kings College London (2016) *Diversity and Governance*, www.kcl.ac.uk/hr/diversity/bias.aspx.

Kohli, R. (2014) 'Unpacking internalised racism: teachers of color striving for racially just classrooms', *Race, Ethnicity and Education* 17(3): 346–87.

Lalani, M., Metcalf, H., Tufekci, L., Corley, A., Rolfe, H., and George A. (2014) *How Place Influences Employment Outcomes for Ethnic Minorities*, York: Joseph Rowntree Foundation.

Leonardo, Z. (2009) *Race, Whiteness and Education*, London and New York: Routledge.

Lereya, S., Winsper, C., Heron, J., Lewis, G., Gunnell, D., Fisher, H., and Wolke, D. (2013) 'Being bullied during childhood and the prospective pathways to self-harm in late adolescence', *Journal of the American Academy of Child Adolescent and Psychiatry* 52(6): 608-18.

Lewis, R. (2000) *Feminist Postcolonial Theory*, London: Routledge.

Li, Y. (2015) 'Ethnic minority unemployment in hard times', in C. Alexander and J. Arday (eds), *Aiming Higher: Race, Inequality and Diversity in the Academy*, London: Runnymede Trust, pp 35–8.

Lindley, J. (2009) 'The over-education of UK immigrants and minority ethnic groups: evidence from the Labour Force Survey', *Economic Educational Review* 28: 80–9.

Lipman, P. (2012) 'Neoliberalism, urbanism, race and equity in mathematics education', *Journal of Mathematics Urban Education* 5(2): 6–17.

Loke, G. (2015) 'Breaking the race inequality cycle in education: a change of focus is needed to break the statistical groundhog day', in C. Alexander and J. Arday (eds), *Aiming Higher: Race, Inequality and Diversity in Higher Education*, London: Runnymede, pp 42–4.

Longhi, S., Nicoletti, C. and Platt, L. (2013) 'Explained and unexplained wage gaps across the main ethno-religious groups in Great Britain', *Oxford Economic Papers* 65(2): 471–93.

Lowery, B., Knowles, E. and Unzueta, M. (2006) 'Framing inequity safely: whites' motivated perceptions of racial privilege', *Personality and Social Psychology Bulletin* 33(9): 1237–50.

Macdonald, A. (2014) *Not for People Like Me? Under-represented Groups in Science, Technology and Engineering*, South East Physics Network: WISE.

Macpherson, W. (1999) *Report of the Stephen Lawrence Enquiry*, London: The Stationery Office.

Marx, S. and Pennington, J. (2010) 'Pedagogies of critical race theory: experimentations with preservice teachers', *International Journal of Qualitative Studies in Education* 16(1): 91–110.

McGee, E.O. and Martin, D.B. (2011) 'From the hood to being hooded: case study of a Black male PhD', *Journal of African American Males in Education* 2(1): 46–65.

McIntosh, P. (1989) 'White privilege: unpacking the invisible knapsack', http://nationalseedproject.org/white-privilege-unpacking-the-invisible-knapsack.

McIntyre, A. (1997) *Making Meaning of Whiteness: Exploring Racial Identity and White Teachers*, New York: University of New York.

Menash, J. (1995) 'Journey to work and job search characteristics of the urban poor', *Transportation* 22(1): 1–19.

Milner, R., Pabon, A., Woodson, A. and McGee, E. (2013) 'Teacher education and black male students in the US', *Multidisciplinary Journal of Educational Research* 3(3): 235–63.

Morgan, M. (2011) *Supporting Postgraduate Taught Students into and out of Study*, London: Higher Education Academy.

Morgan, M. (2014) 'Widening the participation in postgraduate education: delivering targeted and sustainable support for postgraduate STEM students'. Paper presented at *The Future of Postgraduate Education 2014*, Inside Government, London, 12 June.

Morrison, T. (1993) *The Nobel Lecture*, Princeton, NJ: Princeton University Press.

Moss-Racusin, C., Dovidio, J., Brescoll, V., Graham, M. and Handelsman, J. (2012) 'Science faculty's subtle gender biases favour male students', *Proceedings of the National Academy of Sciences for the United States of America* 109(41): 16474–9.

Myers, M., McGhee, D. and Bhopal, K. (2010) 'At the crossroads – Gypsy, Roma and Traveller parents' perceptions of education, protection and social change – observations from a pilot study', *Race, Ethnicity and Education* 13(4): 533–48.

Myers, M. and Bhopal, K. (2015) 'Racism and bullying in rural primary schools in England: protecting White identities post-Macpherson', *British Journal of Sociology of Education* 38(2): 125–43 (doi: 10.1080/01425692.2015.1073099).

National Audit Office (2015) 'Equality, diversity and inclusion in the civil service', https://www.nao.org.uk/wp-content/uploads/2015/06/Equality-diversity-andinclusion-in-the-civil-service.pdf.

National Centre for Education Statistics (2016) 'Characteristics of postsecondary students', http://nces.ed.gov/programs/coe/indicator_csb.asp.

National Society for the Prevention of Cruelty to Children (2015) 'Bullying and cyberbullying: facts and statistics', https://www.nspcc.org.uk/preventing-abuse/child-abuse-and-neglect/bullying-and-cyberbullying/bullying-cyberbullying-statistics/.

National Student Survey (2014) *Findings and Trends*, London: NSS

National Union of Students (2011) *Race for Equality: A Report of the Experiences of Black Students in Further and Higher Education*, London: National Union of Students, http://www.nus.org.uk/en/news/race-for-equality/

National Union of Students Connect (2016) 'Why is my curriculum white? Decolonising the academy', 10 February, http://www.nusconnect.org.uk/articles/why-is-my-curriculum-white-decolonising-the-academy.

National Union of Teachers (2011) *National Traveller Education Survey: A Summary of Findings*, https://www.teachers.org.uk/files/national-traveller-education-survey-report.pdf.

Newsday (2016) 'Donald Trump speech, debates and campaign quotes', http://www.newsday.com/news/nation/donald-trump-speech-debates-and-campaign-quotes-1.11206532.

Newsweek Europe (2015) 'Why are Black Americans at greater risk of being poor?' 8 October, http://europe.newsweek.com/why-are-black-americans-greater-risk-being-poor-331423?rm+eu.

Noden, P., Shiner, M. and Modood, T. (2014) 'University offer rates for candidates from different ethnic categories', *Oxford Review of Education* 40(3): 349–69.

NSPCC (2014) *What Children Are Telling Us about Bullying*, London: NSPCC.

Office for National Statistics (ONS) (2012) *A Comparison of the 2011 Census and Labour Force Survey, Labour Market Indicators*, https://tinyurl.com/ycb5z4sp

ONS (2014a) 2011 *Census Analysis: Social and Economic Characteristics by Length of Residence of Migrant Populations in England and Wales*, London: ONS.

ONS (2014b) *What Does the 2011 Census Tell Us About the Characteristics of Gypsy or Irish Travellers in England and Wales?* London: ONS.

ONS (2015) *Census Data Analysis: Ethnicity and the Labour Market for England, Scotland and Wales*, London: ONS.

OFSTED (Office for Standards in Education) (2012) *No Place for Bullying*, London: OFSTED.

Olssen, M. (2000) 'Ethical liberalism, education and the "New Right"', *Journal of Education Policy* 15(5): 481–508.

Osler, A. (2016) *Human Rights and Schooling: An Ethical Framework for Teaching for Social Justice*, Colombia University: Teachers College Press.

Osler, A. and Starkey, H. (2010) *Teachers, Human Rights and Education*, Stoke on Trent: Trentham.

Owen, D. (2013) *Evidence on the Experience of Poverty by People from Ethnic Minority Groups in Wales*, York: Joseph Rowntree Foundation.

Özbilgin, M. and Tatli, A. (2011) 'Mapping out the field of equality and diversity: rise of individualism and voluntarism', *Human Relations* 64(9): 1229–52.

Parel, K. and Boliver, V. (2014) 'Ethnicity trumps school background as a predictor of admission to elite UK universities', *Economics of Higher Education*, 9 May, http://economicsofhe. org/2014/05/09/ethnicity-trumps-schoolbackground-as-a-predictor-of-admission-to-elite-ukuniversities/.

Patacchini, E. and Zenou, Y. (2011) 'Neighbourhood effects and parental involvement in the intergenerational transmission of education', *Journal of Science* 51: 987–1013.

Pearce, S. (2014) 'Dealing with racist incidents: what do beginning teachers learn from schools?' *Race, Ethnicity and Education* 17(3): 388–406.

Pew Research (2015) 'Black child poverty rate holds steady even as other groups see declines', 14 July, http://www.pewresearch. org/fact-tank/2015/07/14/black-child-poverty-rate-holds-steady-even-as-other-groups-see-declines/.

Pilkington, A. (2013) 'The interacting dynamics of institutional racism in higher education', *Race, Ethnicity and Education* 16(2): 225–45.

Preston, J. (2008) 'Protect and survive: whiteness and middle class family in civil defence pedagogies', *Journal of Education Policy* 23(5): 469–82.

Preston, J. and Bhopal, K. (2011) 'Conclusion: Intersectional theories and "race". From toolkit to "mash-up"', in K. Bhopal and J. Preston (eds), *Intersectionality and 'Race' in Education*, London: Routledge, pp 213–20.

Quality Curriculum Agency (1998) *The National Curriculum*, London: DfE.

Quillian, L. (2006) 'New approaches to understanding racial prejudice and discrimination', *Annual Review of Sociology* 32(1): 299–328.

Race on the Agenda (2012) *Do Free Schools Help to Build a More Equal Society?* London: ROTA.

Rafferty, A. (2012) 'Ethnic penalties in graduate level over-education, unemployment and wages: evidence from Britain', *Work, Employment and Society* 26: 987–1006.

Reardon, S., Baker, R. and Klasik, D. (2012) 'Race, income and enrolment patterns in highly selective colleges 1982–2004', https://cepa.stanford.edu/sites/default/files/race%20income%20%26%20selective%20college%20enrollment%20august%203%202012.pdf.

Reay, D. (2005) 'Doing the dirty work of social class? Mothers' work in support of their children's schooling', in M. Glucksmann, L. Pettinger and J. West (eds), *A New Sociology of Work*, Oxford: Blackwell.

Reay, D. (2015) 'Time to change: bringing Oxbridge into the 21st century', in C. Alexander and J. Arday (eds), *Aiming Higher: Race, Inequality and Diversity in Higher Education*, London: Runnymede, pp 19–21.

Research Councils UK (2016) *Equality and Diversity Statement*, http://www.rcuk.ac.uk/funding/diversity/.

Richardson, J.T.E. (2015) 'The under-attainment of ethnic minority students in UK higher education: what we know and what we don't know', *Journal of Further and Higher Education* 39: 278–91.

Riggins, S. (2001) *The Language and Politics of Othering*, Thousand Oaks, CA: Sage.

Robertson, S. (2005) *'Remaking the World': Neo-liberalism and the Transformation of Education and Teachers' Labour*, Bristol: Centre for Globalisation, Education and Societies, http://www.bris.ac.uk/education/people/academicStaff/edslr/publications/17slr/.

Roediger, D. (1999) *The Wages of Whiteness*, New York: Verso.

Roediger, D. (2005) *Working towards Whiteness: How American Immigrants Became White*, New York: New York University Press.

Rothstein, R. (2014) 'The colour-blind bind: focusing college-student recruitment on poor neighborhoods can overlook middle-class African Americans entitled to affirmative action', *American Prospect* 25(4): 70–5.

Royal College of General Practitioners (2013) *Improving Access to Healthcare for Gypsies and Travellers*, London: RCGC.

Runnymede Trust (2010) *Widening Participation and Race Equality*, London: Runnymede.

Runnymede Trust (2015) *The 2015 Budget: Effects on Black and Minority Ethnic People*, London: Runnymede.

Saul, J. (2005) *The Collapse of Globalism and the Reinvention of the World*, Camberwell: Viking.

Sears, D. and Henry, P. (2003) 'The origins of symbolic racism', *Journal of Personality and Social Psychology* 85(2): 259–75.

Simpson, L., Purdam, K., Tajar, A., Fieldhouse, E., Gavalas, V., Tranmer, M., Pritchard, J. and Dorling, D. (2006) *Ethnic Minority Populations and the Labour Market: An Analysis of the 1991 and 2001 Census*, London: Department for Work and Pensions.

Skiba, R.J., Michael, R.S., Nardo, A.C. and Peterson, R.L. (2002) 'The color of discipline: sources of racial and gender disproportionality in school punishment', *Urban Review* 34: 317–42.

Sleeter, C. (2011) 'Becoming white: reinterpreting a family story by putting race back into the picture', *Race, Ethnicity and Education* 14(4): 421–33.

Small, M., Harding, D. and Lamont, M (2010) 'Reconsidering children and poverty', *Annals of the American Academy of Political and Social Science* 629(1): 6–27.

Social Mobility and Child Poverty Commission (2015) *State of the Nation: Social Mobility and Child Poverty in Great Britain*, London: The Stationery Office.

Solomon, R.P., Portelli, J., Daniel, B. and Campbell, A. (2005) 'The discourse of denial: how white teacher candidates construct race, racism and white privilege', *Race Ethnicity and Education* 8(2): 147–69.

Stevens, M.L. (2007) *Creating a Class: College Admissions and the Education of Elites*, Cambridge, MA: Harvard University Press.

Sue, D., Capodilupo, C., Torino, G., Bucceri, J., Holder, A., Nadal, K. and Esquilin, M. (2007) 'Racial micro aggressions in everyday life', *American Psychologist* 62 (4): 273–86.

Sutton Trust (2014) 'Summer schools aim to dispel state schools teacher misconceptions', 11 August, https://www.suttontrust. com/newsarchive/summer-schools-aim-dispel-state-school-teachers-oxbridge-misconceptions/.

Swann Report (1985) *Education for all: Report of the Committee of Inquiry into the Education of Children from Ethnic Minority Groups*, London: HMSO.

Taylor, E. (2000) 'Convergence in the backlash against affirmative action: Washington state and initiative 200', *Teachers College Record* 201(3): 539–60.

The Telegraph (2016) 'Teaching children British values is an act of "cultural supremacism"', 28 March, http://www.telegraph. co.uk/news/2016/03/28/teaching-children-fundamental-british-values-is-act-of-cultural/.

Times Higher Education (2016a) 'BME students more likely to do Masters not research', 14 July, https://www. timeshighereducation.com/news/bme-students-more-likely-do-masters-not-research.

Times Higher Education (2016b) 'Four universities to trial name blind applications', 8 September, https://www. timeshighereducation.com/news/four-universities-trial-name-blind-applications.

Times Higher Education (2016c) 'David Cameron: name blind UCAS forms will reduce bias', 26 October, https://www. timeshighereducation.com/news/david-cameron-name-blind-ucas-forms-will-address-race-bias.

Trades Union Congress (2013) *Review of the Equality Duty*, London: TUC.

Trades Union Congress (2015) 'Press release: number of black and Asian workers in low-paid jobs up by 13 per cent since 2011, TUC report reveals', https://www.tuc.org.uk/ economic-issues/equality-issues/blackworkers/campaigns/ number-black-and-asianworkers-low-paid-jobs.

Trade Unions Congress (2016) 'Black workers with degrees earn less than white counterparts', https://www.tuc.org.uk/ equality-issues/black-workers/labour-market/black-workers-degrees-earn-quarter-less-white.

United Nations Human Rights Council (2013) *Global Trends Report*, Geneva, Switzerland: UNHRC.

UNCRC (2008) *Safe to Learn. United Nations Convention on the Rights of the Child*, London: DCSF.

UNDP (2005) *Human Development Report 2005: International Cooperation at a Crossroads: Aid Trade and Security in an Unequal World*, New York: UNDP, http://hdr.undp.org/reports/global/2005.

University and College Union (2016) *The Experiences of Black and Minority Ethnic Staff in Further and Higher Education*, London: UCU.

Universities UK (2013a) *The Funding Environment for Universities in the UK*, London: Universities UK.

Universities UK (2013b) *Postgraduate Taught Education: The Funding Challenge*, London: Universities UK.

US Census Bureau (2014) *Statistics on Poverty and Ethnicity*, https://www.census.gov/.

US Department of Education, Office of Elementary and Secondary Education, Consolidated State Performance Report, 2013–14. See *Digest of Education Statistics* (2015) https://nces.ed.gov/pubs2016/2016014.pdf.

US Department of Education, National Centre for Education Statistics, Integrated Postsecondary Education Data System (IPEDS), spring 2014, Fall enrolment component, https://nces.ed.gov/pubs2015/2015098.pdf.

US National Centre for Children in Poverty (2014), http://www.nccp.org/publications/pub_1145.html.

US News (2016) 'Achievement gap between white and black students still gaping', 13 January, https://www.usnews.com/news/blogs/data-mine/2016/01/13/achievement-gap-between-white-and-black-students-still-gaping.

Vizard, P., Karagiannaki, E., Cunliffe, K., Fitzgerald, A., Obolenskaya, P., Thompson, S., Grollman, C. and Lupton, R. (2015) 'The changing anatomy of economic inequality in London (2007–2013)', http://sticerd.lse.ac.uk/dps/case/spcc/rr06.pdf.

Warikoo, N. (2016) *The Diversity Bargain: And Other Dimensions of Race, Admissions, and Meritocracy at Elite Universities*, Chicago, IL: University of Chicago Press.

Washington, M. (1987) *Invented Lives: Narratives of Black Women, 1860–1960*, Garden City, NY: Doubleday.

Washington Post (2015) 'Who really supports Donald Trump?', 15 December, https://www.washingtonpost.com/news/the-fix/wp/2015/12/15/who-really-supports-donald-trump-ted-cruz-ben-carson-marco-rubio-and-jeb-bush-in-5-charts/.

Weekes-Bernard, D. (2007) *School Choice and Ethnic Segregation*, London: Runnymede.

Wheatstone, R. (2015) 'More than 900 British children identified as potential extremists at risk of radicalisation from ISIS and terror groups', http://www.mirror.co.uk/news/uk-news/more-900-british-children-identified-6080066.

Yumiko, A. (2009) *Homeless Children and Youth*, New York: Colombia University National Centre for Child Poverty.

Zuccotti, C.V. (2015) 'Do parents matter? Revisiting ethnic penalties in occupation among second generation ethnic minorities in England and Wales', *Sociology* 49: 229–51.

Zwysen, W. and Longhi, S. (2016) *Employment and Earnings Gap in the Early Careers of Ethnic Minority Graduates*, UCL, London: Centre for Research on Race and Ethnicity.

Index

Index